主 编 宋 艳（Maggie）

I can speak Chinese

我能说中国话

编者 雷若琳（Sophie）

万 黎（Sunny）

温晓宁（Sophy）

翻译 黄 烨（Kitty）

1

上海交通大学出版社

SHANGHAI JIAO TONG UNIVERSITY PRESS

内容提要

  本系列教材是一套针对零起点的成年汉语学习者编写的汉语教程，共三册，每册三个级别，每个级别十八课。本系列教材按照《国际汉语教学通用课程大纲》的要求，打破传统教材格局，以生词讲解为切入点，将词语使用技巧公式化，并配以大量例句，使入门阶段的汉语学习更易懂、易掌握。除纸质教材外，本教材配有相应的数字化辅助教学资源供学习者使用，配合使用可有效提高学习效果。

图书在版编目（CIP）数据

我能说，中国话.1 / 宋艳主编. —上海：上海交
通大学出版社，2016
ISBN 978－7－313－16145－1

Ⅰ.①我… Ⅱ.①宋… Ⅲ.①汉语—对外汉语教学—
教材 Ⅳ.①H195.4

中国版本图书馆 CIP 数据核字（2016）第 273215 号

我能说，中国话1

主 编：宋 艳
出版发行：上海交通大学出版社   地 址：上海市番禺路 951 号
邮政编码：200030   电 话：021－64071208
出 版 人：郑益慧
印 制：常熟市文化印刷有限公司 经 销：全国新华书店
开 本：710 mm×1000 mm 1/16 印 张：20.75
字 数：302 千字
版 次：2016 年 11 月第 1 版   印 次：2016 年 11 月第 1 次印刷
书 号：ISBN 978－7－313－16145－1/H
定 价：128.00 元

随着中国经济的蓬勃发展及中国国际地位的提升,汉语学习已不仅仅是个人的兴趣爱好,而越来越成为重要的工具语言。

如今的汉语学习者大抵可分为两大类:一类为来华脱产学习的学院派留学生;另一类则为因工作或生活需要而学习的实用派学习者。

市面上传统汉语教材或以留学生活为背景,或以日常生活场景为划分,或局限于地域性语言特色,或过多灌输专业语法知识,教材形式也多为冗长的课文配以大篇幅的生词表。此类教材已越来越无法满足广大学习者的学习需求。

本教材作者团队凭借十年以上的一线教学经验,打破传统教材格局,标新立异,扬长避短,以简洁、精练、通俗易懂的英语作为媒介语言进行解释说明,以生词讲解为切入点,将词语使用技巧公式化,再配以大量例句,使入门阶段的汉语学习更加易理解、易吸收、易掌握。

以"a little bit"为例,在汉语中可译为"有点儿"或"一点儿",但用法却大不相同。本书未对其语法特点做过多讲解,仅用两个公式比较说明其相同点与不同点,即"有点儿 + adj."和"adj. + 一点儿"。"有点儿 + adj."用于不太满意时;"adj. + 一点儿"则用于比较。例如:"这个房间有点(儿)小,有大一点(儿)的吗?"这种讲解轻理论、重实用,言简意赅,相信能帮助学习者更加有效地分辨和记忆。

本教材的编写团队成员,皆为具有十年以上一线教学经验的对外汉语教师,他们直接了解学习者在学习中经常遇到的问题及学习需求,并以有效解决问题和满足实际需求作为编写宗旨。他们面对传统汉语教材越来越无法满足广大学习者学习需求的局面，勇于创新，探索新模式，历经一年半时间创作了本系列教材。

本教材为全英文教材，为本书担任翻译的是旅美多年的黄烨女士。黄女士多年的对外汉语教学经历最大程度地保证了媒介语言精准适用。

本套系列教材属于初级教程，共分九个级别，共三册，每册三个级别，每个级别18课，每册54课，内容由易到难，循序渐进，有助于稳步提高学习者的汉语水平。课文标题以E508为例，E意为Elementary（初级），5为级别标号，08为课文标号。

本教材的生词皆选取自HSK汉语水平考试大纲，并加以适当引申，初级教材三册书生词量共1 020个，可达到HSK考试三级水平。

本教材不仅可以作为汉语学习者的学习用书，也可作为汉语教学者的培训用书，因书中所选生词皆为教师日常教学中遇到的问题，本教材对这些问题给予了充分的解释和说明。

最后，向对本教材的出版给予过无私帮助的各界朋友表示感谢。衷心希望本套教材能够对大家学好汉语有所帮助。限于能力，不足之处请大家批评指正。

宋　艳

2016 年 8 月

With the vigorous development of economy and the rise of international status of China, learning Chinese is no longer just a personal interest, but becomes an increasingly important tool language.

Nowadays, Chinese learners probably can be roughly divided into two groups: full-time students and the learners to meet the needs of communication in daily life and work.

Traditional Chinese teaching materials, usually set in the scenes of overseas study or daily life, only focused on the regional language features, with too much professional grammars and lengthy texts and new words. Such teaching materials have been unable to meet the requirements of the majority of learners.

The author team of this series of textbooks, with nearly 20 years of teaching experience, aims to make the Chinese learning easy and simple to grasp by breaking the traditional teaching patterns, explaining the new words in brief and concise English and formulizing the usage of the words with great examples.

Illustrate the phrase "a little bit" as an example. It can be translated as "a little" in Chinese but it differs a lot in usage. We can explain the similarities and differences by comparing two formulas "a little bit + adj." and "adj. + a little bit". "A little bit + adj." is to show one is less satisfied; "adj. + a little bit" is used to compare. For example, "This room is a little bit small, do you have a bigger one?" This method gives much more attention to the practice rather than the theory, and it can help learners distinguish and memorize the new words more efficiently.

The compiling team consists of the Chinese teachers with a decade of teaching experiences. The profound knowledge of the problems students often encountered in the daily study makes the compiling more practical and efficient. To meet the market's large appetite for the qualified Chinese teaching textbooks, all the compiling team members strive for the new modes, creating this series of textbooks in one year and a half.

This series of textbooks, written in English, is translated by Ms. Huang Ye who has lived overseas for years. Her years' experience in teaching Chinese as a foreign language guarantees the accuracy of the media language to the greatest extent.

This series of textbooks, divided into nine levels, a total of three books, each book including three levels, each level 18 classes, one book 54 classes, can help the students improve their English step by step. For example, the title E 508, E represents "elementary", 5 "the grade label", and 08 "the text label".

New words in this series of textbooks are stem from the HSK test syllables with some extensions. The amount of the new words is 1,020, reaching HSK Level 3.

This series of textbooks cannot only be used as textbooks, but also as teachers' books. We give a detailed account of the new words in this series of textbooks.

Finally, the author would like to extend her sincere gratitude and acknowledgement to her friends for their dedicated help and wish this series of the textbooks could be of help to all the Chinese learners. If there exist any inadequacies, the author welcomes all the suggestions and advice.

Maggie（宋艳）

目录
Contents

一 级

二　　级

三 级

一

级

The Chinese Phonetics

Welcome to our *ChineseAny* podcast series teaching Chinese. This is Level One, Lesson One. In today's lesson, we will introduce the Chinese phonetics. The phonetic unit of Chinese is a syllable, with each syllable usually represented by one character.

A Chinese syllable is usually composed of an **initial**, a **final** and a **tone**. The initial is a consonant that begins the syllable, and the final covers the rest of the syllable.

> (Tone)
> syllable = initial + final

There are 21 initials, 36 finals and 4 basic tones in the standard Chinese.

> 21 initials
> 36 finals
> 4 tones

Now we will learn the syllables and the pronunciation rules of each syllable.

Firstly, let's see the initial, "*shēngmǔ 声母*".

b	p	m	f	d	t	n	l
g	k	h					
j	q	x					
z	c	s					
zh	ch	sh	r				

> 声母
> [shēngmǔ]   initial

Let's learn the finals, "*yùnmǔ 韵母*".

A final is a simple or compound vowel or a vowel plus a nasal consonant. Some syllables may have no initial consonant. For example, "*ài 爱*" means "love", but every syllable has a vowel. Let's see the finals now.

韵母		
[yùnmǔ]		final

a	o	e	er	i	-i(zi)	-i(zhi)	u	ü
ai	ei	ao	ou	an	en	ang	eng	ong
ia	ie	iao	iou(iu)	ian	in	iang	ing	iong
ua	uo	uai	uei(ui)	uan	uen(un)	uang	ueng	
üe	üan	ün						

After learning the initials and finals, let's see the tones. There are four basic tones in the standard Chinese. They are indicated by following tone-marks：the first tone(ˉ), the second tone(ˊ), the third tone(ˇ), and the fourth tone(ˋ).

The 1st tone	The 2nd tone
The 3rd tone	The 4th tone

Except four basic tones, there are some syllables that lost their original tones and are pronounced soft and short, and they are called "neutral tone".

The neutral tone do not have any tone mark, e. g. "*māma 妈妈*", "*bàba 爸爸*". When a syllable is pronounced in different tones, it has different meanings.

Māma	妈妈
Bàba	爸爸

OK, please look at the following diagrams of tones.

For example,

ā

ā = a1

1st tone

- 5(high)

2nd tone

- 4(mid-high)

4th tone

- 3(middle)

3rd tone

- 2(mid-low)

- 1(low)

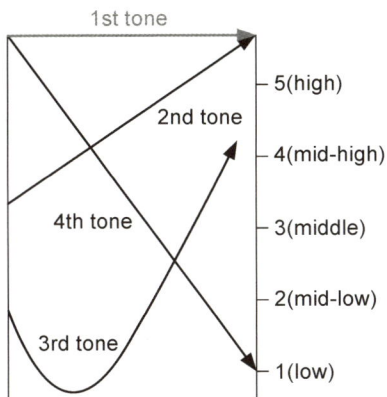

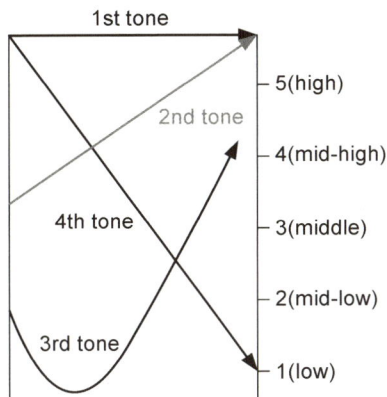

Tone	Mark	Note
1st	mā	It is pronounced high and flat.
2nd	má	From middle rises up to high, it sounds just like to ask someone's question.
3rd	mǎ	From mid-low falls to low, and then rises to mid-high.
4th	mà	Starts at the top, then falls sharp and strong to the bottom, and sounds like an angry tone.

á

á = a2

1st tone

- 5(high)

2nd tone

- 4(mid-high)

4th tone

- 3(middle)

3rd tone

- 2(mid-low)

- 1(low)

Tone	Mark	Note
1st	mā	It is pronounced high and flat.
2nd	má	From middle rises up to high, it sounds just like to ask someone's question.
3rd	mǎ	From mid-low falls to low, and then rises to mid-high.
4th	mà	Starts at the top, then falls sharp and strong to the bottom, and sounds like an angry tone.

ǎ

ǎ = a3

1st tone

2nd tone

4th tone

3rd tone

- 5(high)
- 4(mid-high)
- 3(middle)
- 2(mid-low)
- 1(low)

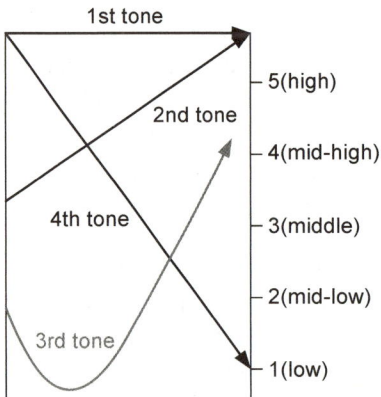

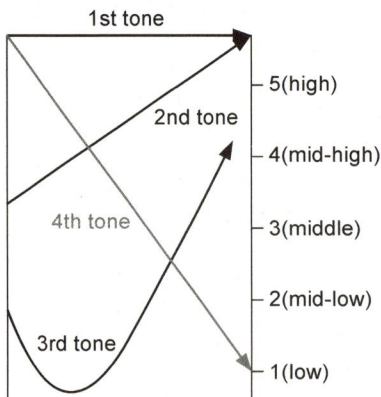

Tone	Mark	Note
1st	mā	It is pronounced high and flat.
2nd	má	From middle rises up to high, it sounds just like to ask someone's question.
3rd	mǎ	From mid-low falls to low, and then rises to mid-high.
4th	mà	Starts at the top, then falls sharp and strong to the bottom, and sounds like an angry tone.

à

à = a4

1st tone

2nd tone

4th tone

3rd tone

- 5(high)
- 4(mid-high)
- 3(middle)
- 2(mid-low)
- 1(low)

Tone	Mark	Note
1st	mā	It is pronounced high and flat.
2nd	má	From middle rises up to high, it sounds just like to ask someone's question.
3rd	mǎ	From mid-low falls to low, and then rises to mid-high.
4th	mà	Starts at the top, then falls sharp and strong to the bottom, and sounds like an angry tone.

There are some points to note about Chinese tones.

1. Tone changes

① When there are two third-tone syllables together, the 1st one should be pronounced with the 2nd tone. But the syllable is still marked in the 3rd tone.

e. g. *nǐ hǎo* 你好 is pronounced *ní hǎo* 你好 ,

shuǐguǒ 水果 is pronounced *shuí guǒ* 水果 .

> ˇ + ˇ = ´ + ˇ
> ● [nǐhǎo] = [níhǎo]
>   你好 hello
> ● [shuǐguǒ] = [shuíguǒ]
>   水果 fruit

② **Change of tone of "bù 不"**

"*bù* 不" means *no or not*.

"*bù* 不" is the 4th tone, and it changes to the 2nd tone when before a syllable in the 4th tone.

e. g. *bù qù* 不去→*bú qù* 不去 ,

bù shì 不是→*bú shì* 不是.

> 不[b**ù**] →不[b**ú**] + 4th tone
> [b**ù** qù]→[b**ú** qù] 不去 no go
> [b**ù** shì]→[b**ú** shì] 不是 no

When "*bù* 不" before a syllable in the 1st, 2nd, or 3rd tone, it is still pronounced in the 4th tone.

e. g. *bù gāo* 不高→*bù gāo* 不高 ,

bù lái 不来→*bù lái* 不来 ,

bù hǎo 不好→*bù hǎo* 不好.

> 不[b**ù**] + 1st/2nd/3rd tone
>
> [b**ù** gāo] 不高 not tall
> [b**ù** lái] 不来 not come
> [b**ù** hǎo] 不好 no good

③ **Change of tone of "yī 一"**

"yī 一" as an ordinary number means *one*, we will learn it later.

[yī] 一 one

"yī 一" is the 1st tone, when before a syllable in the 4th tone, it is pronounced in the 2nd tone.

e. g. *yī gè* 一个 → *yí gè* 一个 ,
　　　yī cì 一次 → *yí cì* 一次 .

一[yī] → 一[yí] + 4th tone
[yī gè] → [yí gè]
一个 one thing
[yī cì] → [yí cì]
一次 one time

When "yī 一" before a syllable in the 1st, 2nd, or 3rd tone, it is pronounced in the 4th tone.

e. g. *yī tiān* 一天 → *yì tiān* 一天 ,
　　　yī píng 一瓶 → *yì píng* 一瓶 ,
　　　yī qǐ 一起 → *yì qǐ* 一起 .

一[yī] + 1st/2nd/3rd tone
[yī tiān] → [yì tiān] 一天
one day
[yī píng] → [yì píng] 一瓶
one bottle
[yī qǐ] → [yì qǐ] 一起
together

2. Tone mark

① When there is only one vowel in a syllable, the tone mark is put above the vowel.

yī	láng	qù
wǒ	zhǒu	xùn

Note：If the mark is above the vowel "i", the dot of "i" is omitted.

e. g. *nǐ* 你 , *yīng* 英 , *bí* 鼻 , *cì* 次 .

nǐ	yīng
bí	cì

② When there are two or more than two vowels in the final of a syllable, the tone mark is put on the main vowel.

e. g. *bái* 白 , *kuài* 快.

yāo	bái
kuài	zhǒu

③ When a syllable beginning with a, o, e is attached to another syllable, we may use the dividing mark " ' " between the two syllables.

e. g. *Xī 'ān 西安* , *wǎn 'ān 晚安*.

Xī'ān 西安

wǎn'ān 晚安

Great, after the tone mark, now let's learn the spelling rules.

① When a syllable starts with " *i* ",
(*i ia ie iao iu ian in iang ing iong*)
"i" should be written as "y".
(yi ya ye yao you yin yang ying yong).
"i" is replaced by "y".

i	yi	ian	yan
ia	ya	in	yin
ie	ye	iu	yu
iao	yao	iang	yang
ing	ying	iong	yong

② When a syllable starts with "*u* ",
(*u ua uo uai uei uan uen uang ueng*)
"u" should be written as "w".
(wu wa wo wai wei wan wang weng).
"u" is replaced by "w".

u	wu	uan	wan
ua	wa	uen	wen
uo	wo	uang	wang
uai	wai	ueng	weng
uei	wei		

③ When a syllable starts with "*ü* ", (*ü üe üan ün*)
"ü" should be written as "y"
(yu yue yuan yun).

ü	yu	üe	yue
üan	yuan	ün	yun

④ When "*zh ch sh r z c s*" is stranded for a syllable, it should be written as "zhi chi shi ri zi ci si".

zh	zhi	z	zi
ch	chi	c	ci
sh	shi	s	si
r	ri		

⑤ When "*j*", "*q*", "*x*" are put before "ü" or a final begins with "ü", the two dots in "ü" are dropped.

j	q	x
ju	qu	xu

but it's still pronounced as "ü", not "u".
e.g. *júzi* 桔子, *xuéxí* 学习.

[júzi] 桔子 orange
[xuéxí] 学习 study

⑥ When a syllable is formed by "*iou*", "*uei*" or "*uen*" after an initial, the "o" and "e" in the finals should be omitted.

iou	uei	uen
iu	ui	un

e.g. *duèi* →duì, *guèi* →guì.

[d**uèi**] → [d**uì**]
对 right
[g**uèi**] → [g**uì**]
贵 expensive

⑦ The final "**er**" alone from a syllable
never follows an initial.

e. g. *értóng* 儿童 , *ěrduō* 耳朵 .

[***ér*** tóng] 儿童 child
[***ěr*** duo] 耳朵 ear

⑧ The final "**er**" sometimes can be
attached to another final to form a
retroflex final. In spelling , "r" is added
to the end of the original final.

e. g. *zhèr* 这儿 , *nǎr* 哪儿 .

[zhè***r***] 这儿 here
[nǎ***r***] 哪儿 where

Great , so that wraps up today's lesson. Hope you learned something
from this. Download our app to access our Chinese lessons. Remember
you can learn Chinese anywhere , anytime with ***ChineseAny***.

The Pronouns

Welcome to our ***ChineseAny*** podcast series teaching Chinese. This is Level One, Lesson Two. In our last lesson, we introduced the Chinese phonetics to you. If you are not familiar with them, we encourage you to listen to Lesson One again to get a handle on them. Today let's use them to learn how to say Pronouns in Chinese.

The 1st word, "I, ME".

In Chinese we say *wǒ* 我, the 3rd tone, *wǒ* 我.

我
[wǒ]
I, me

The 2nd word, "YOU".

In Chinese we say *nǐ* 你, the 3rd tone, *nǐ* 你.

你
[nǐ]
you

The 3rd word, "SHE, HE, IT".

In Chinese we say *tā*, the 1st tone, *tā* 他/她/它.

她/他/它
[tā]
she/he/it

The pronunciation for "SHE, HE, IT" are same in Chinese, but the Chinese characters are different. Let's see the difference.

The 1st "*tā 她*" is for the female. You can see the left part of the character is like a sitting woman, who is feeding a baby.

女　𠂉

The 2nd "*tā 他*" is for the male. You can see the left part of this character is like a standing man.

他　亻

The 3rd "*tā 它*" is for objects. We use it for animals, plants, and other objects, except for persons.

它

OK, now let's learn how to say the plural form of "*wǒ 我*", "*nǐ 你*" and "*tā 他*". We just need to add "*mén 们*" after them to make the plural form.

So "*wǒmen 我们*" means "we, us".

"*nǐmen 你们*" means "you people, you all".

"*tāmen 他们*" means "they, them".

For possessive pronouns, we just need to add "*de 的*" after them.

So MY is "*wǒ de 我的*"　　　OUR is "*wǒmen de 我们的*"

YOUR is "*nǐ de 你的*"　　　YOUR is "*nǐmen de 你们的*"

HER/HIS/ITS is "*tā de 他的*"　　THERE is "*tāmen de 他们的*"

Let's see a form to summarize today's lesson.

I (me)	[wǒ] 我	We (us)	[wǒmen] 我们
You (you)	[nǐ] 你	You (you)	[nǐmen] 你们
It	[tā] 它	They (them)	[tāmen] 它们
My	[wǒ de] 我的	Our	[wǒmen de] 我们的
Your	[nǐ de] 你的	Your	[nǐmen de] 你们的
Her/his/its	[tā de] 他的	Their	[tāmen de] 他们的

Great, so that wraps up today's lesson. I hope you learned something from this. Download our app to access our Chinese lessons. Remember you can learn Chinese anywhere, anytime with **ChineseAny**.

◯ **Word List**

		们 [men]	的 [de]
我 [wǒ]		我们 [wǒmen]	我的 [wǒde]
你 [nǐ]		你们 [nǐmen]	你的 [nǐde]
他／她／它 [tā]		他们 [tāmen]	他的 [tāde]

◯ **Notes**

① **The plural form of the Pronoun：**

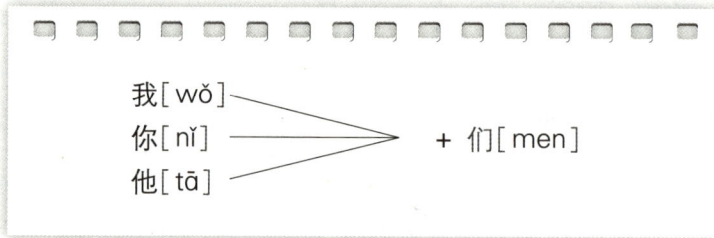

我 [wǒ]
你 [nǐ]   + 们 [men]
他 [tā]

② **The possessive pronouns：**

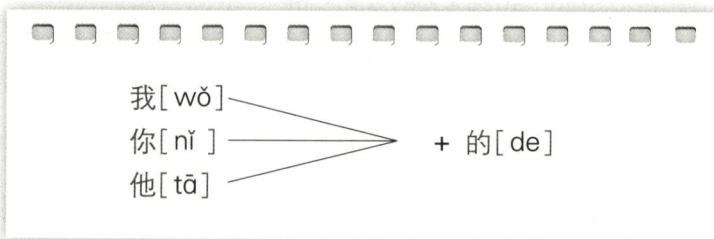

我 [wǒ]
你 [nǐ]   + 的 [de]
他 [tā]

Quiz

I. Pronunciation.

1. Please choose the initials or finals you heard.

1) A. b   B. p

2) A. ai   B. ao

3) A. n   B. l

4) A. an   B. en

2. Please choose the Pinyin you heard.

1) A. kèqi   B. kètí

2) A. zúqiú   B. tīqiú

3) A. chāoshì   B. cháoshī

4) A. kùzi   B. dùzi

II. Form sentences.

1. <u>tā</u>   <u>bàba</u>   <u>de</u>
   1   2   3

_____

2. <u>de</u>   <u>wǒ</u>   <u>māma</u>
   1   2   3

_____

3. <u>wǒ</u>   <u>de</u>   <u>men</u>
   1   2   3

_____

4. <u>de</u>   <u>bàba</u>   <u>nǐmen</u>
   1   2   3

_____

III. Please translate the following sentences into Chinese.

1. His mother. _____   2. Their father. _____

3. Our mother. _____   4. Your father. _____

Hello

Welcome to Level One Lesson Three of our *ChineseAny* podcast series teaching Chinese. Today we will learn how to greet in Chinese. There are four words and two common conversation words.

The 1st word, "*nǐ hǎo* 你好", Hello！
"*nǐ* 你" means "you", "*hǎo* 好" means "good", "*nǐ hǎo* 你好" means "I hope you are good". Chinese people often use "hello, hi" for greeting.

> 你好
> [nǐ hǎo]
> hello

The 2nd word, "*nín hǎo* 您好".
"*nín* 您" is the polite way of "*nǐ* 你", we use "*nín* 您" towards the people that you respect like people older than you or people whose position is higher than yours.

> 您好
> [nín hǎo]
> hello

So we say "*nǐ hǎo* 你好" to our friends and kids.

But we say "*nín hǎo* 您好" to our parents, teachers or bosses.

The 3rd word, "*xièxie* 谢谢", means "thanks". You can also add "*nǐ* 你" after it. "*xièxie nǐ* 谢谢你" means thank you！

Pay attention to the 2nd "*xiè* 谢" which would be pronounced in neutral tone.

> 谢谢
> [xièxie]
> thank

The 4th word is the reply for "*xièxie* 谢谢", "*bú kèqi* 不客气".

> A：谢谢你[xièxie nǐ]
> Thank you.
> B：不客气[bú kèqi]
> You are welcome.

"*bù* 不" means "not, do not, does not, will not". It's a very common native word in Chinese.

> 不
> [bù]
> not

We always use it before **verbs** and **adjectives**.

> 不 + verb/adj.
> [bù]

One thing we need to pay attention to is that "*bù* 不" will change to the 2nd tone when it meets the 4th tone.

> 不 { [bù] + 1st/2nd/3rd tone
>   [bú] + 4th tone

So we say "*bú kèqi*", but not "*bù kèqi*", since the "*kè*" in "*kèqi*" is 4th tone. "*kèqi* 客气" means "to be polite", "*bú kèqi* 不客气" means "don't need to be polite". It also means "you are welcome".

Great, so that wraps up today's lesson. Hope you learned something from this. Thanks for taking time to learn Chinese with me today. Please don't forget to do the exercise and practice more.

Word List

Main Vocabulary			
您[nín] you	好[hǎo] good, fine	谢谢[xièxie] Thank you.	不客气[bú kèqi] You're welcome.
Additional Vocabulary			
不[bù] no, not	客气[kèqi] polite		

Notes

① **You：**

Normal way	Polite way
你[nǐ]	您[nín]

e.g.　你好。[Nǐ hǎo]　Hello.
　　　您好。[Nín hǎo]　Hello.

② **不[bù] + verb/adj.**

e.g.　不客气。[Bú kèqi]　You're welcome.
　　　不好。[Bù hǎo]　Not Good.

Quiz

I. Pronunciation.

1. Please choose the initials or finals you heard.

1) A. b   B. d

2) A. ye   B. ya

3) A. ai   B. ei

4) A. üe   B. ün

2. Please choose the Pinyin you heard.

1) A. bú tuì   B. bú duì

2) A. guānxì   B. guān jī

3) A. duìmiàn   B. duìbiān

4) A. hǎoxiàng   B. hǎoxiāng

II. Form sentences.

1. guānxì   tāmen   de   hǎo   hěn
   1   2   3   4   5

   _____

2. men   duì   wǒ
   1   2   3

   _____

3. hǎo   māma   Judy
   1   2   3

   _____

4. qǐ   duì   bu
   1   2   3

   _____

III. Please translate the following sentences into Chinese.

1. Hello, Sophie.

_____

2. Yes, their relationship is good.

_____

3. Our relationship is not good.

_____

4. A: Sorry.

_____

B: It does not matter.

_____

Sorry

Welcome to Level One, Lesson Four of our **ChineseAny** podcast series teaching Chinese. Today we will learn three sentences and four words. Are you ready?

Today's 1st sentence: *duì bùqǐ* 对不起！Sorry！

"*duì* 对" means "right", "*bùqǐ* 不起" means "can't afford". I can't afford I'm right, "*duì bùqǐ* 对不起"！

对 + 不起
[duì] + [bùqǐ]
right   can't afford

The 2nd sentence: *méi guānxi* 没关系！It doesn't matter！

"*méi* 没" means "do not have", "*guānxi* 关系" means "relationship". It has no relationship with you.

没 + 关系
[méi] + [guānxi]
don't have   relationship

The 3rd sentence: *zài jiàn* 再见. See you！Goodbye！

再见
[zài jiàn]
goodbye

"*zài* 再" means "again", "*jiàn* 见" means to meet, to see. To see you again, "*zài jiàn* 再见"！

再 + 见
[zài] + [jiàn]
again   see

From the three sentences, let's learn four new words.

First, "*duì* 对", right.

e.g. Sophie is right. *Suǒfēi duì* 索菲对！

You are not right. *Nǐ búduì* 你不对！

Second, "*guānxi* 关系", relationship, "*guānxi* 关系"

e.g. Our relationship "*wǒmen de guānxi* 我们的关系"

Their relationship "*tāmen de guānxi* 他们的关系"

Third, "*zài* 再", again. We often use this before a **verb** to express doing something again. "*zài jiàn* 再见"

再 + verb

[*zài*]

again

Fourth, "*jiàn* 见", to meet, to see, "*jiàn* 见"

e.g. See you, "*jiàn nǐ* 见你"; see him, "*jiàn tā* 见他";

meet them, "*jiàn tāmén* 见她们".

In Lesson 3, we learned "*bù* 不", it means "**NOT**".

Let's try to make some simple sentences with "*bù* 不" and please pay attention to the tone changes. "not good", "*bù hǎo* 不好"; "not right", "*bú duì* 不对"; "do not see", "*bú jiàn* 不见"; "do not thank", *bú xiè* 不谢"; "do not see them", *bú jiàn tāmen* 不见他们！"

Great, so that wraps up today's lesson. Download our app to access our Chinese lessons. Remember, you can learn Chinese anywhere, anytime with **ChineseAny**.

Word List

Main Vocabulary		
对不起[duì buqǐ] sorry	没关系[méi guānxi] It does not matter	再见[zài jiàn] bye-bye
Additional Vocabulary		
对[duì] right, correct	没[méi] not	关系[guānxi] relationship
再[zài] again	见[jiàn] to meet, to see	

Notes

① **Negative sentence：不[bù] + verb/adj.**

　e. g.　不见［bú jiàn］　not meet　　不谢［bú xiè］　You're welcome.

　　　　不好［bù hǎo］　not good　　不对［bú duì］　not correct

② **Tone changes：不[bù]**

　　　［bù］ +1st/2nd/3rd tone　　　不好［bù hǎo］

　　　［bú］ + 4th tone　　　　　不谢［bú xiè］

Quiz

I. Pronunciation.

　1. Please choose the initials or finals you heard.

　　1）A. zh　　　　　　　B. z

　　2）A. in　　　　　　　B. ing

3) A. r B. y

4) A. uo B. ou

2. Please choose the Pinyin you heard.

1) A. zhùyì B. zhǔyì

2) A. měitiān B. méiyǒu

3) A. zàijiàn B. zàiqián

4) A. guānxì B. guānxīn

II. Form sentences.

1. jiàn   wǒ   bú   tā
   1   2   3   4

   _____

2. xièxie   de   nǐ   māma
   1   2   3   4

   _____

3. nǐ   xièxie   wǒ   jiàn
   1   2   3   4

   _____

4. tā   māma   jiàn   de   nǐ
   1   2   3   4   5

   _____

III. Please translate the following sentences into Chinese.

1. Thank you, Sophie.

   _____

2. You are welcome.

   _____

3. I do not meet her.

   _____

4. Goodbye, Mom.

   _____

Good Morning

Welcome to Level One, Lesson Five of our **ChineseAny** podcast series teaching Chinese. Today we will learn five time expressions, from morning to evening.

The 1st one, "*zǎoshàng* 早上", early morning. "*zǎoshàng* 早上", normally we use it to refer to **"6 am — 8 am"**.
"*Zǎo* 早" means "early".

早上
[zǎoshàng]
early morning

The 2nd one, "*shàngwǔ* 上午", late morning. "*shàngwǔ* 上午": from **8 am — 12 pm**.
"*Shàng* 上" in Chinese means "up or on".

上午
[shàngwǔ]
late morning

The 3rd one, "*zhōngwǔ* 中午", noon. "*zhōngwǔ* 中午": from **12 pm — 1 pm**.
"*Zhōng* 中" means "middle".

中午
[zhōngwǔ]
noon

The 4th one, "*xiàwǔ* 下午",afternoon. "*xiàwǔ* 下午": from **1 pm — 6 pm**.
"*Xià* 下" in Chinese usually means "down".

下午
[xiàwǔ]
afternoon

The last one, "*wǎnshàng 晚上*": evening.
"*wǎnshàng 晚上*": from 6 pm — 10 pm.
"*Wǎn 晚*" means "late or evening".

晚上
[wǎnshàng]
evening

By now you should all be quite familiar with "*nǐ hǎo 你好*".
Let's learn a few new greetings depending on the time of day.
Good morning, "*zǎoshàng hǎo 早上好！*"
Good afternoon, "*xiàwǔ hǎo 下午好*"
Good evening, "*wǎnshàng hǎo 晚上好*"

OK, now let's try to put together what we know so far.
Good morning, Sophie — "*Zǎoshàng hǎo 早上好，索菲！*"
Good afternoon, you guys — "*Nǐmen xiàwǔ hǎo 你们下午好！*"

OK, there are 5 time expressions in today's lesson, plus "*hǎo 好*" after them, It forms a greeting that can be used at certain times of the day. Also, please remember these two common adjectives*zǎo 早*, early；*wǎn 晚*, late.

Great, so that wraps up today's lesson. Hope you learned something from this. Download our app to access our Chinese lessons. Remember you can learn Chinese anywhere, anytime with **ChineseAny**.

Q **Word List**

Main Vocabulary		
早上 [zǎoshang] early morning	上午 [shàngwǔ] late morning	中午 [zhōngwǔ] noon
下午 [xiàwǔ] afternoon	晚上 [wǎnshang] evening	

Additional Vocabulary		
早 [zǎo] early	上 [shàng] on, up	中 [zhōng] middle
下 [xià] down, under	晚 [wǎn] late	

Notes

① **Greetings depending on the time of day：**

Time + 好 [hǎo]

e.g. 早上好！[Zǎoshang hǎo]   Good morning.

早！[Zǎo]   Good morning.

下午好！[Xiàwǔ hǎo]   Good afternoon.

晚上好！[Wǎnshang hǎo]   Good evening.

Quiz

I. Pronunciation.

  1. Please choose the initials or finals you heard.

    1) A. wā   B. yā

    2) A. hǎo   B. zǎo

    3) A. hàn   B. gàn

    4) A. huì   B. guì

  2. Please choose the Pinyin you heard.

    1) A. kànjiàn   B. zàijiàn

    2) A. xièxie   B. xiézi

    3) A. bú shì   B. bùzhì

4) A. jiǎnjiè   B. jiànjiē

II. Form sentences.

1. <u>wǒ</u>   <u>jiàn</u>   <u>zhōngwǔ</u>   <u>tā</u>
    1   2   3   4

---

2. <u>hǎo</u>   <u>zǎoshang</u>   <u>bù</u>
    1   2   3

---

3. <u>wǎnshang</u>   <u>hǎo</u>   <u>nǐmen</u>
      1   2   3

---

4. <u>māma</u>   <u>wǒ</u>   <u>jiàn</u>   <u>tāde</u>   <u>zhōngwǔ</u>
    1   2   3   4   5

III. Please translate the following sentences into Chinese.

1. Good morning, Sophie.

---

2. I do not meet your mother in the morning.

---

3. Sorry, the evening is not good.

---

4. We don't meet in the morning.

YES or NO Question

Welcome to Level One, Lesson Six of **ChineseAny** podcast series teaching Chinese. Today we will learn three new words, specifically two particles and one adverb. In grammar, a particle is a word or a part of a word that has a grammatical purpose but often has little or no meaning. Let's start.

The 1st particle is "*ma* 吗", neutral tone. We put it at the end of a sentence, and it can turn a statement into a "YES" or "NO" question.

吗
[ma]
question mark　particle

So if the literal translation of "*nǐhǎo* 你好" means "you are good", "*nǐ hǎo ma?* 你好吗?" is a question, so it means "are you good?" And that's also used to ask "How are you?" It is used between people who have already met each other or who haven't seen each other for a long time.

你好 ⇨ 你好吗?
[nǐhǎo] [nǐhǎo ma]
hello　　How are you?

OK, let's move to one of the most common answers to "How are you?", which is "*wǒ hěn hǎo.* 我很好", "I'm very good!"

So, the 2nd word for today is "*hěn 很*".
"*hěn 很*" means "very". Although they have the same meaning, "*hěn 很*" is less intense than "very", so you tend to use "*hěn 很*" far more often in Chinese than "very" in English.
The way to say "I'm good" in Chinese is "wó hěn hǎo 我很好"
"You are early" in Chinese is "nǐ hěn zǎo 你很早"
"He is polite" in Chinese is "tā hěn kèqi 他很客气"

很
[hěn]
very   adverb

OK, now let's move to our last word, a particle "*ne 呢*" in neutral tone, which we also put at the end of a sentence. Its meaning is "how about".

呢
[ne]
how about   particle

So "how about you?" or "and you?" in Chinese would be "*nǐ ne 你呢？*"

Pronoun + 呢
[ne]
how about + pronoun

Good, so let's put together what we know so far. Please try to translate the following sentences into Chinese.

- 你好，索菲，你好吗？［Nǐ hǎo, Sophie, nǐ hǎo ma］
  Hello, Sophie, How are you?

- 我很好，谢谢，你呢？［Wǒ hěn hǎo, xièxie, nǐ ne］
  I'm Good, thank you, and you?

- 你的妈妈好吗？［Nǐ de māma hǎo ma］

How is your mom?

● 他们的关系好吗?［Tāmen de guānxi hǎo ma］
Is their relationship good?

The last thing I need to point out is the difference between "*hěn bù* 很不" and "*bù hěn* 不很".
"*hěn bù hǎo* 很不好" means "very bad".
"*bù hěn hǎo* 不很好" means "not very good, but it's OK".

Great, so that wraps up today's lesson. Remember, you can learn Chinese anywhere, anytime with **ChineseAny**.

Word List

Main Vocabulary		
很［hěn］ very	吗［ma］ particle	呢［ne］ particle

Notes

① **Yes or No question**：

Statement sentence + 吗［ma］?

e.g. 你好吗?［Nǐ hǎo ma］ How are you?

你的妈妈好吗?［Nǐ de māma hǎo ma］ How is your mom?

② **很**［hěn］ **+ adj.**：

e. g.　我很好。［Wǒ hěn hǎo］　I'm fine.

　　　他很客气。［Tā hěn kèqi］　He is very polite.

③ **Pronoun +** 呢［ne］?

e. g.　你呢? ［Nǐ ne］　How about you?

　　　他呢? ［Tā ne］　And him?

④ **很不**［hěn bù］ **+ adj.** : totally negative.

　不很［bù hěn］ **+ adj.** : partly negative.

e. g.　很不好。［Hěn bù hǎo］　It is very bad.

　　　不很好。［Bù hěn hǎo］　It is not very good.

Quiz

I. Pronunciation.

　1. Please choose the initials or finals you heard.

　　1) A. guò　　　　　　　B. gòu

　　2) A. sān　　　　　　　B. shān

　　3) A. māo　　　　　　　B. miāo

　　4) A. lèi　　　　　　　　B. nèi

　2. Please choose the Pinyin you heard.

　　1) A. zhàogù　　　　　　B. zhàngfu

　　2) A. huǒshān　　　　　　B. huànsàn

　　3) A. máobìng　　　　　　B. máobǐ

　　4) A. Guǎngdōng　　　　　B. Guǎngzhōu

II. Form sentences.

　1. <u>nǐ</u>　<u>hǎo</u>　<u>māma</u>　<u>ma?</u>
　　　1　　2　　　3　　　4

2. <u>de</u>   <u>bàba</u>   <u>hěn</u>   **Sophie**   <u>kèqi</u>
  1   2   3   4   5

3. <u>bù</u>   <u>tāmen</u>   <u>hěn</u>   <u>de</u>   <u>guānxì</u>   <u>hǎo</u>
  1   2   3   4   5   6

4. <u>xiàwǔ</u>   <u>wǒmen</u>   <u>jiàn</u>
  1   2   3

III. Please translate the following sentences into Chinese.

1. She is very good.

2. How are you?

3. I will see you in the morning.

4. Their relationship is very bad.

I'm Maggie

Welcome to Level One, Lesson Seven of our **ChineseAny** podcast series teaching Chinese. Today we will learn five new words, one verb and four nouns. Let's have a look.

是[shì] to be	先生[xiānsheng] Mr./husband	太太[tàitai] Mrs./wife
老师[lǎoshī] teacher	学生[xuésheng] student	

Now let's learn how to use them.

xiānshēng 先生 means both "Mr. and husband". *tàitai* 太太 means both "Mrs. and wife".

In Chinese, we put the family name in front of the address to form the prefixes like Mr., Mrs., Ms., or the title.

Family name + { Title / Address form }

So "Mr. White" in Chinese should be *White xiānshēng* 先生.
"Mrs. White" in Chinese should be *White tàitai* 太太.
"Teacher Maggie" should be *Maggie lǎoshī* 老师.
This is quite different from English, so please pay attention to the differences.

"*shì 是*" is a very useful verb in Chinese. It means "to be (am/is/are)". It is always followed by a noun.

是
[shì]
to be   verb

When you use it, please remember two points:

① We normally use nationality, name, relationship and job after "*shì 是*".

是
[shì] +
{
nationality
name
relationship
job
}

② When describing someone or something, we use adjectives such as good, polite, or tired, we can't use "*shì 是*". Instead, we must use "*hěn 很*".

S. + to be + adj
S. + 很 + *adj.* ×
　　[hěn]
S. + 是 + *adj.*
　　[shì]

For example:

"I'm good" in Chinese should be "*Wǒ hěn hǎo 我很好*", but not "*wǒ shì hǎo 我是好*".

我 很 好 √
[wǒ hěn hǎo]
我 是 好 ×
[wǒ shì hǎo]

35

"You are early" in Chinese should be "*nǐ hěn zǎo 你很早*", but not "*nǐ shì zǎo 你是早*".

你 很 早 √
[nǐ hěn zǎo]
你 是 早 ×
[nǐ shì zǎo]

Great, so let's do some practice with the vocabularies and put together what we have known so far.

We know how to say "I", "*wǒ 我*", and we know how to say "your" "*nǐ de 你的*".

So with that in mind, how would you say "I am your teacher"? "*Wǒ shì nǐ de lǎoshī 我是你的老师*".

I   am your teacher
我   是 你的 老师
[wǒ shì nǐde lǎoshī]

Now, let's do some more practice. I'll ask you to translate the following sentences from English to Chinese.

● 他是我的先生。
[Tā shì wǒ de xiānshēng]
He is my husband.

● 她是我的太太。
[Tā shì wǒ de tàitai]
She is my wife.

● 玛姬是我们的老师。
[Mǎjī shì wǒmen de lǎoshī]
Maggie is our teacher.

● 你好，我是索菲。
[Nǐ hǎo, wǒ shì Suǒfēi]
Hello, I'm Sophie.

● 汤姆不是我的学生。

[Tāngmǔ bú shì wǒ de xuéshēng]

Tom is not my student.

● 你是玛丽吗?

[Nǐ shì Mǎlì ma]

Are you Mary?

Great, so that wraps up today's lesson. Hope you have learned something useful. Take a look at the summary on our vocabulary page. You can also find the full transcript which comes with the video. Also, we have prepared lots of exercise to review and test what you have learned.

Word List

Main Vocabulary		
怎么[zěnme] how to	路[lù] road/bus number	师傅[shīfu] Sir(driver)

Notes

① **怎么**[zěnme] **+ verb**:**how to**

e. g. ● 这个汉语怎么说? [Zhège Hànyǔ zěnme shuō]

How do you say this in Chinese?

● 中国饭怎么做? [Zhōngguó fàn zěnme zuò]

How to cook Chinese food?

● 请问，南京路怎么走？［Qǐng wèn Nánjīng lù zěnme zǒu］

Excuse me, how do I get to Nanjing road?

● 你们怎么去北京？［Nǐmen zěnme qù Běijīng］

How do you go to Beijing?

Quiz

I. Pronunciation.

1. Please choose the initials or finals you heard.

1) A. lún   B. yún

2) A. bù   B. pù

3) A. é   B. è

4) A. huài   B. guài

2. Please choose the Pinyin you heard.

1) A. zěnme   B. zhème

2) A. shàngcè   B. shàng chē

3) A. shīfu   B. shūfu

4) A. xìqǔ   B. xīqǔ

II. Form sentences.

1.   qǐng   shīfu   zhège   wèn   lù   zǒu   zěnme
     1   2   3   4   5   6   7

2.   zěnme   zhège   Hànzì   shuō
     1   2   3   4

3.   mǎi   diànyǐng   zěnme   piào
     1   2   3   4

4. <u>Zhōngguó</u>   <u>zhège</u>   <u>cài</u>   <u>zuò</u>   <u>zènme</u>
    1   2   3   4   5

_____

III. Please translate the following sentences into Chinese.

1. How do you know her phone number?

_____

2. I am on the way to work.

_____

3. I like to go to work on foot.

_____

4. How do you study Chinese?

_____

Nationality

Welcome to Level One, Lesson Eight of our **ChineseAny** podcast series teaching Mandarin Chinese. Today let's learn how to express your nationality and its corresponding language. We will focus on learning three words.

The 1st one is "*guó 国*", country. In Chinese, we often use it to name a country.

"*Zhōngguó 中国*", China.

"*Měiguó 美国*", the United States.

国
[guó]
Country   noun

The names of some countries are transliterated, such as "*xīnjiāpō, 新加坡*", Singapore. "*éluósī 俄罗斯*" Russia. But most do not follow this rule.

We've listed the names of a few countries, please recite them.

中国	[Zhōngguó]	China
英国	[Yīngguó]	Britain
德国	[Déguó]	Germany
新加坡	[Xīnjiāpō]	Singapore
意大利	[Yìdàlì]	Italy
西班牙	[Xībānyá]	Spain
美国	[Měiguó]	The United States

（续表）

法国	[Fǎguó]	France
泰国	[Tàiguó]	Thailand
俄罗斯	[É luósī]	Russia
丹麦	[Dānmài]	Denmark
加拿大	[Jiānádà]	Canada

OK, today's 2nd word is "*rén* 人", person or people.

So could you tell me how to say Chinese people in Chinese?

人
[rén]
Person　　noun

Yes, you are right, Chinese people in Chinese is "*Zhōngguó rén* 中国人". Putting the word "*rén* 人" after the country's name to describe people from that country.

Country Name ＋ 人
　　　　　　　　[rén]

The last word of today's lesson is "*yǔ* 语", language.
Normally, we put it after the country's name to express the language of that country with the exception of "Chinese".

语
[yǔ]
Language　Noun

Chinese is called "*hànyǔ* 汉语" rather than "中国语".

Country Name ＋ 语
　　　　　　　　[yǔ]

Let's try to translate the following sentences into Chinese to review what we have known so far.

- 她是我的汉语老师。
  [Tā shì wǒ de Hànyǔ lǎoshī]
  She is my Chinese teacher.

- 我是中国人。
  [Wǒ shì Zhōngguó rén]
  I'm a Chinese.

- 你的太太是中国人吗?
  [Nǐ de tàitai shì Zhōngguó rén ma]
  Is your wife Chinese?

- 你们好,我是汉语老师。
  [Nǐmén hǎo, wǒ shì Hànyǔ lǎoshī]
  Hello, I'm Maggie, and I'm a Chinese teacher.

OK, so that wraps up today's lesson. Hope you have learned something today. Please listen to our lessons again or download our app to access our Chinese lessons. Remember, you can learn Chinese anywhere, anytime with **ChineseAny**.

Word List

Main Vocabulary		
国 [guó] country	人 [rén] person/people	语 [yǔ] language
Additional Vocabulary		
汉语 [Hànyǔ] Chinese Mandarin		

Notes

① **Country name + 人**[rén]：**the people from that country**

e. g. ● 我的老师是中国人。[Wǒ de lǎoshī shì Zhōngguó rén]
My teacher is Chinese.

● 他的太太是美国人。[Tā de tàitai shì Měiguó rén]
His wife is American.

● 你的学生是英国人吗？[Nǐ de xuésheng shì Yīngguó rén ma]
Is your student English?

② **Country Name + 语**[yǔ]：**the language of that country**

e. g. ● 意大利语 [Yìdàlì yǔ]　　Italian

● 俄罗斯语 [Éluósī yǔ]　　Russian

● 法语 [Fǎ yǔ]　　French

Quiz

I. Pronunciation.

1. Please choose the initials or finals you heard.

　　1) A. shū　　　　　　　　B. sū

　　2) A. zhàn　　　　　　　B. zàn

　　3) A. lóu　　　　　　　　B. liú

　　4) A. huì　　　　　　　　B. kuì

2. Please choose the Pinyin you heard.

　　1) A. Hànyǔ　　　　　　　B. Hányǔ

　　2) A. Hànzì　　　　　　　B. hànzi

　　3) A. háishì　　　　　　　B. huánshì

4) A. fángjiān   B. fāngbiàn

II. Form sentences.

1. rén   nǐ   shì   ma   Zhōngguó
   1   2   3   4   5

2. Hànyǔ   tā   shì   de   lǎoshī   wǒmen
   1   2   3   4   5   6

3. wǒ   Zhōngguó   xiānsheng   bú   rén   shì
   1   2   3   4   5   6

4. Hànyǔ   tā   shì   lǎoshī   tàitai
   1   2   3   4   5

III. Please translate the following sentences into Chinese.

1. Sorry，she is not my Chinese teacher.

2. Thank you，Teacher Sophie. You are a good teacher.

3. She is my husband's English teacher.

4. Her Chinese is very good.

I'm Busy

Welcome to Level One, Lesson Nine of our **ChineseAny** podcast series teaching Chinese. In our last eight lessons, we have learned how to greet someone, how to express your name, and how to express your nationality. Hope you're getting a sense of the Chinese language.

In today's lesson, we will learn three adjectives.
Busy, "*máng* 忙", in the 2nd tone.
Tired, "*lèi* 累", in the 4th tone.
Hungry, "*è* 饿", in the 4th tone.

忙 [máng]	be busy
累 [lèi]	be tired
饿 [è]	be hungry

In Chinese, when we use an adjective to describe the situation of somebody or something, we typically use the following pattern:
sb./sth. + hěn 很 + adj.
But not **sb./sth. + shì 是 + adj.** Remember, we have already known that we can only use the name, nationality, job and relationship after "*shì 是*".

sb./sth. + hěn 很 + adjective.	√
sb./sth. + shì 是 + adjective.	✗

Now please pay attention to this point, We ONLY use this pattern for statements. But for questions, you don't have to use "*hěn 很*", unless you really need to emphasize your point, similar to the usage of "very" in English.

OK, let's follow the pattern：*Sb./sth. + hěn 很 + adj* to practice using these three adjectives in Chinese.

No.1, the statement sentences：

① He is busy. *Tā hěn máng 他很忙*.

② We are hungry. *Wǒmen hěn è 我们很饿*.

③ You are tired. *Nǐ hěn lèi 你很累*.

No.2, the Yes or No question：

① Are you busy?　"*Nǐ máng ma 你忙吗？*"

But "*nǐ hěn máng ma 你很忙吗？*" means "Are you **VERY** busy?"

② Is your student tired?　"*Nǐ de xuéshēng lèi ma 你的学生累吗？*"

But "*Nǐ de xuéshēng hěn lèi ma 你的学生很累吗？*" means "Is your student **VERY** tired?"

③ Are they hungry?　"*Tāmen è ma 他们饿吗？*"

But "*Tāmen hěn è ma 他们很饿吗？*" means "Are they **VERY** hungry?"

No.3, negative sentences：

In negative sentences, normally we don't use "*hěn 很*" either. When you would like to make the statements in a less intense tone, you may also use "*hěn 很*" to achieve this.

For example：

① I'm not busy. In Chinese it would be "*wǒ bù máng. 我不忙*".

But "*wǒ bù hěn máng 我不很忙*" means "I'm not **VERY** busy".

② She is not tired. In Chinese it would be "*tā bú lèi 他不累*".

But "*tā bù hěn lèi 他不很累*" means "She is not **VERY** tired".

③ My husband is not hungry. In Chinese it would be "*wǒde xiānshēng bú è 我的先生不饿*". But "*wǒde xiānshēng bù hěn è 我的先生不很饿*" means "My husband is not **VERY** hungry".

OK, that's all for today's lesson. Hope you have learned something today. Download our app to access our lessons and exercises that we've designed to help you review and test your comprehension. Remember, you can learn Chinese anywhere, anytime with **ChineseAny**.

◖ **Word List**

Main Vocabulary		
忙[máng] be busy	累[lèi] be tired	饿[è] be hungry

◖ **Notes**

① **sb./sth. + 很[hěn] + adjective：**

e.g. ● 他很忙。[Tā hěn máng] He is very busy.

　　● 我们很饿。[Wǒmen hěn è] We are very hungry.

　　● 张老师很好。[Zhāng lǎoshī hěn hǎo] Teacher Zhang is very good.

② **sb./sth. + 不[bù] + adjective：**

e.g. ● 我不忙。[Wǒ bù máng] I'm not busy.

　　● 他不累。[Tā bú lèi] He is not tired.

　　● 她的先生不好。[Tā de xiānsheng bù hǎo] Her husband is not good.

③ **sb./sth. + adjective + 吗[ma]：**

e.g. ● 你的学生累吗?[Nǐ de xuésheng lèi ma] Is your student tired?

● 他们饿吗? ［Tāmen è ma］ Are they hungry?

● 你的老师好吗? ［Nǐ de lǎoshī hǎo ma］ Is your teacher good?

Quiz

I. Pronunciation.

  1. Please choose the initials or finals you heard.

    1) A. mèi   B. miè

    2) A. wǎn   B. wǎng

    3) A. yín   B. yíng

    4) A. zài   B. sài

  2. Please choose the Pinyin you heard.

    1) A. zhùhè   B. zhúgè

    2) A. fángzi   B. bǎngzi

    3) A. tángshuǐ   B. tàngzuǐ

    4) A. lèi le   B. lè le

II. Form sentences.

  1. <u>wǒ</u>   <u>máng</u>   <u>xiānsheng</u>   <u>hěn</u>
      1   2   3   4

    _____

  2. <u>tāmen</u>   <u>lèi</u>   <u>de</u>   <u>hěn</u>   <u>lǎoshī</u>
      1   2   3   4   5

    _____

  3. <u>wǒ</u>   <u>nǐ</u>   <u>è</u>   <u>ne</u>   <u>bú</u>
      1   2   3   4   5

    _____

  4. <u>nǐmen</u>   <u>ma</u>   <u>máng</u>
      1   2   3

    _____

III. Please translate the following sentences into Chinese.

1. I am not tired, thank you.

_____

2. She is my Chinese teacher, and she is very busy.

_____

3. I am very hungry, and you?

_____

4. His wife is very busy.

_____

We're All Happy

Welcome to Level One, Lesson Ten of our **ChineseAny** podcast series teaching Mandarin Chinese. Today we will learn three new words. Let's start now.

The 1st one is "*gāoxìng* 高兴", "be glad", adjective.

You may say "*hěn gāoxìng* 很高兴", be happy; or "*bù gāoxìng* 不高兴", not happy.

> 高兴
> [gāoxing]
> be glad   *adjective*

The 2nd word is an adverb.

Before we learn it, please pay attention to this important point. In Chinese, we always use the format **adverb + verb or adjective**, always! Please keep this in mind when you use it.

$$\text{adverb} + \begin{cases} \textit{verb} \\ \textit{adjective} \end{cases}$$

OK, let's learn our 2nd new word, which is an adverb. "*yě* 也", means "also, too".

> 也
> [yě]
> also, too   adverb

For example：

- 我也很好。［Wǒ yě hěn hǎo］
  I'm good，too.
- 他也是美国人。［Tā yě shì Měiguó rén］
  He is American，too.

The 3rd word is "*dōu 都*"，which means "all or both".

> 都
> ［dōu］
> all，both   adverb

It's an adverb，too. The subject before "*dōu 都*" should be "the plural form".

> plural form ＋都＋verb
> ［dōu］

For example：

- 我们都很累。［Wǒmen dōu hěn lèi］
  We are all tired.
- 你们都是我的学生。［Nǐmen dōu shì wǒ de xuéshēng］
  You are all my students.

OK，let's memorize some patterns，which will help you more easily make correct sentences.
No.1：**S.** + "*yě 也*" + "*bù 不*" + **Verb/Adj.** means "Not . . . either".

> S. + "也" + "不" + verb/adj.
> ［yě］　　［bù］

For example：

- 我们也不饿。［Wǒmen yě bú è］
  We are not hungry either.

- 我们也不是中国人。[Wǒmen yě bú shì Zhōngguó rén]
  We are not Chinese either.

No.2：S. + "*yě 也*" + "*dōu 都*" + **verb/adj.** , means "all/both … too/also".

> S. + ""也"" + ""都"" + verb/adj.
>   [yě]   [dōu]

For example：
- 他们也都是汉语老师。[Tāmen yě dōu shì Hànyǔ lǎoshī]
  They are all Chinese teachers, too.
- 他们也都很忙。[Tāmen yě dōu hěn máng]
  They are all busy, too.

No.3：S. + "*bù 不*" + "*dōu 都*" + **verb/adj.** , means "not all …".

> S. + ""不"" + ""都"" + verb/adj.
>   [bù]   [dōu]

For example：
- 我们不都是老师。[Wǒmen bù dōu shì lǎoshī]
  Not all of us are teachers.
- 他们不都很高兴。[Tāmen bù dōu hěn gāoxìng]
  Not all of them are happy.

No.4：S. + "*dōu 都*" + "*bù 不*" + **verb/adj.** , means "all not …".

> S. + ""都"" + ""不"" + verb/adj.
>   [dōu]   [bù]

For example：
- 我们都不是老师。[Wǒmen dōu bùshì lǎoshī]
  None of us are teachers.

● 他们都不高兴。［Tāmen dōu bù gāoxìng］

None of us are happy.

Let's review all of the sentences, and please think about differences between them.

● 我也很好。

［Wǒ yě hěn hǎo］

I'm good too.

● 他也是美国人。

［Tā yě shì Měiguó rén］

He is also an American.

● 我们也不饿。

［Wǒmen yě bú è］

We are not hungry, either.

● 我们也不是中国人。

［Wǒmen yě bú shì Zhōngguó rén］

We are not Chinese, either.

● 我们不都是老师。

［Wǒmen bù dōu shì lǎoshī］

Not all of us are teachers.

● 他们不都很高兴。

［Tāmen bù dōu hěn gāoxìng］

Not all of them are glad.

● 我们都很累。

［Wǒmen dōu hěn lèi］

We are all very tired.

● 你们都是我的学生。

［Nǐmen dōu shì wǒ de xuéshēng］

You are all my students.

● 他们也都是汉语老师。

［Tāmen yě dōu shì Hànyǔ lǎoshī］

They are all Chinese teachers, too

● 他们也都很忙！

［Tāmen yě dōu hěn máng］

They are all very busy, too.

● 我们都不是老师。

［Wǒmen dōu bú shì lǎoshī］

None of us is teacher.

● 他们都不高兴。

［Tāmen dōu bù gāoxìng］

None of them is glad.

Hope you have learned something today. Download our app to access our lessons and exercises that we've designed to help you review and test your comprehension. Remember，you can learn Chinese anywhere，anytime with *ChineseAny*.

Word List

Main Vocabulary		
高兴 [gāoxìng] be happy	也 [yě] also/too	都 [dōu] all of/both of

Notes

① **Adv. + verb or adj.**
　　e. g. ● 我们很高兴。[Wǒmen hěn gāoxìng]
　　　　　We are very happy.
　　　　 ● 他也是美国人。[Tā yě shì Měiguó rén]
　　　　　He is also an American.

② **S. + "也 [yě]" + "不 [bù]" + verb/adj. — not . . . either**
　　e. g. ● 我们也不饿。[Wǒmen yě bú è]
　　　　　We are not hungry either.
　　　　 ● 我们也不是中国人。[Wǒmen yě bú shì Zhōngguó rén]
　　　　　We are not Chinese either.

③ **S. + "也 [yě]" + "都 [dōu]" + verb/adj.**
　　e. g. ● 他们也都是汉语老师。[Tāmen yě dōu shì Hànyǔ lǎoshī]

They are all Chinese teachers, too.

● 他们也都很忙。[Tāmen yě dōu hěn máng]
They are all busy too.

④ **S. + "不[bù]" + "都[dōu]" + verb/adj.**

e.g. ● 我们不都是老师。[Wǒmen bù dōu shì lǎoshī]
Not all of us are teachers.

● 他们不都很高兴。[Tāmen bù dōu hěn gāoxìng]
Not all of them are happy.

⑤ **S. + "都[dōu]" + "bù 不" + verb/adj.**

e.g. ● 我们都不是老师。[Wǒmen dōu bú shì lǎoshī]
None of us are teachers.

● 他们都不很高兴。[Tāmen dōu bù hěn gāoxìng]
None of them are happy.

Quiz

I. Pronunciation.

　1. Please choose the initials or finals you heard.

　　1) A. dōu　　　　　　　B. diū

　　2) A. yě　　　　　　　 B. yǎ

　　3) A. dàn　　　　　　　B. dàng

　　4) A. hǎo　　　　　　　B. hǎi

　2. Please choose the Pinyin you heard.

　　1) A. dòuyóu　　　　　 B. dōngyǒng

　　2) A. huānyíng　　　　　B. huánjìng

　　3) A. lājī　　　　　　　 B. lājù

4) A. dǎdǐ   B. dátí

II. Form sentences.

1. <u>gāoxìng</u>   <u>wǒde</u>   <u>lǎoshī</u>   <u>hěn</u>   <u>Hànyǔ</u>
    1   2   3   4   5

_____

2. <u>tāmen</u>   <u>Zhōngguó</u>   <u>bú</u>   <u>shì</u>   <u>dōu</u>   <u>rén</u>
    1   2   3   4   5   6

_____

3. <u>hěn</u>   <u>wǒmen</u>   <u>yě</u>   <u>è</u>
    1   2   3   4

_____

4. <u>nǐmen</u>   <u>bú</u>   <u>lèi</u>   <u>ma</u>   <u>dōu</u>
    1   2   3   4   5

_____

III. Please translate the following sentences into Chinese.

1. All of them are very happy.

_____

2. She is also a Chinese teacher.

_____

3. Their relationship is not good, either.

_____

4. My husband is busy, and I am busy too.

_____

I Like Milk

Welcome to Level One, Lesson Eleven of our **ChineseAny** podcast series teaching Mandarin Chinese. Today we will learn four new words, one verb and three nouns.

The 1st word, "to like", "*xǐhuan* 喜欢".

喜欢
[xǐhuan]
to like   verb

You may add a **noun** or a **verb** after it, which means "to like somebody/something or like to do something".

You may also put the "*hěn* 很" before it, which means "like somebody/something very much".

（很） 喜欢 + { sb./sth.
[hěn] [xǐhuan]   to do sth.

For example：
- 我很喜欢他们。[Wǒ hěn xǐhuān tāmen]
  I like them very much.
- 你喜欢中国吗? [Nǐ xǐhuān Zhōngguó ma]
  Do you like China?
- 你喜欢我吗? [Nǐ xǐhuān wǒ ma]
  Do you like me?
- 对不起,我不喜欢他. [Dùi bu qǐ, wǒ bù xǐhuān tā]

I'm sorry, I don't like him.

OK, now let's learn these three nouns.

① The 1st noun is ," *kāfēi* 咖啡",
   it means "coffee".

② The 2nd noun is "*shuǐ* 水",
   which means "water".

③ The 3rd noun is "*niúnǎi* 牛奶",
   which means "milk".

咖啡 [kāfēi] coffee
水 [shuǐ] water
牛奶 [niúnǎi] milk

Let's do some exercises to review what we have known so far.
Please try to translate them into Chinese.

●我们都喜欢咖啡。
[Wǒmen dōu xǐhuan kāfēi]
We all like coffee.

●我也喜欢牛奶。
[Wǒ yě xǐhuan niúnǎi]
I like milk, too.

●他很不喜欢咖啡。
[Tā hěn bù xǐhuan kāfēi]
He doesn't like coffee very much.

●他们也都不喜欢他们的汉语老师。
[Tāmen yě dōu bù xǐhuan tāmen de Hànyǔ lǎoshī]
All of them don't like their Chinese teachers, either.

Hope you have learned something today. Download our app to access our lessons and exercises to help you review and test your comprehension Remember, you can learn Chinese anywhere, anytime with **ChineseAny**.

Word List

Main Vocabulary		
喜欢[xǐhuan] to like	咖啡[kāfēi] coffee	水[shuǐ] water
牛奶[niúnǎi] milk		
Additional Vocabulary		
牛[niú] cattle	奶[nǎi] milk	

Notes

① **喜欢**[xǐhuan] **+ sb. /sth. :**

　　Statement sentence：subject + 喜欢[xǐhuan] **+ object.**

　　Negative sentence：subject + 不[bù] **+ 喜欢**[xǐhuan] **+ object.**

　　Question sentence：subject + 喜欢[xǐhuan] **+ object?**

　　e. g. ● 我很喜欢我的老师。[Wǒ hěn xǐhuan wǒ de lǎoshī.]

　　　　　I like my teacher very much.

　　　　● 你喜欢你的学生吗？[Nǐ xǐhuan nǐ de xuésheng ma?]

　　　　　Do you like your student?

● 他不喜欢牛奶。［Tā bù xǐhuan niúnǎi］

He does not like milk.

Quiz

I. Pronunciation.

1. Please choose the initials or finals you heard.

1）A. lǎo   B. nǎo

2）A. yù   B. yuè

3）A. lái   B. lèi

4）A. huài   B. kuài

2. Please choose the Pinyin you heard.

1）A. shuìjiào   B. suíbiàn

2）A. xǐhuan   B. xíguàn

3）A. niúnǎi   B. nǎiniú

4）A. wèiwèn   B. wèiwén

II. Form sentences.

1. <u>Zhōngguó</u>   <u>kāfēi</u>   <u>bù</u>   <u>rén</u>   <u>xǐhuan</u>
         1   2   3   4   5

_____

2. <u>xǐhuan</u>   <u>ma</u>   <u>nǐmen</u>   <u>niúnǎi</u>
        1   2   3   4

_____

3. <u>wǒde</u>   <u>yě</u>   <u>lǎoshī</u>   <u>bù</u>   <u>kāfēi</u>   <u>xǐhuan</u>
       1   2   3   4   5   6

_____

4. <u>tāmen</u>   <u>Hànyǔ</u>   <u>hěn</u>   <u>dōu</u>   <u>de</u>   <u>hǎo</u>
       1   2   3   4   5   6

_____

III. Please translate the following sentences into Chinese.

1. I like coffee very much.

_____

2. I like China, and I also like Chinese.

_____

3. They all do not like coffee either.

_____

4. Chinese milk is very good.

_____

I Like Chinese Tea

Welcome to Level One, Lesson Twelve of our **ChineseAny** podcast series teaching Mandarin Chinese. Today we will learn four new words, one verb and three nouns.

The 1st word is "*hē* 喝".

"*hē* 喝" is a **VERB**, which means "to drink". You may put **a type of drink** after it.

> 喝
> [hē]
> to drink   verb

For example：

- "drink water" in Chinese is "*hē shuǐ* 喝水"；
- "drink milk" in Chinese is "*hē niúnǎi* 喝牛奶"；
- "drink coffee" in Chinese is "*hē kāfēi* 喝咖啡".

Let's make some sentences with "*hē* 喝".

- 你喝咖啡吗? [Nǐ hē kāfēi ma]
  Do you drink coffee?
- 我喜欢喝牛奶。[Wǒ xǐhuān hē niúnǎi]
  I like to drink milk.
- 他不喜欢喝咖啡。[Tā bù xǐhuan hē kāfēi]
  He doesn't like to drink coffee.
- 我喝水,你呢? [Wǒ hē shuǐ, nǐ ne]
  I drink water. How about you?

OK, let's learn how to name other drinks.

① The 1st word is "*chá* 茶", it means "tea".

茶
［chá］
tea noun

② The 2nd word is "*píjiǔ* 啤酒", it means "beer". "*jiǔ* 酒" means "wine, alcohol".

you may use "~ + *jiǔ* 酒" to express the different kinds of wine. We will learn them in the future.

啤酒
［píjiǔ］
tea noun

③ The 3rd word is "*suānnǎi* 酸奶", which means "yogurt", "*suān* 酸" means sour. It's an adjective.

"*nǎi* 奶" means "milk". We have learned "*niú nǎi* 牛奶" before. Fermented milk means yogurt "*suānnǎi* 酸奶" in Chinese.

酸奶
［suānnǎi］
yogurt

OK, we have learned that "good" is "*hǎo* 好" and that "to drink" is "*hē* 喝", so we can put "*hǎo* 好" before "*hē* 喝". "*hǎo hē* 好喝" is an **adjective**, which means "good to drink".

好喝
［hǎo hē］
good to drink   adjective

So you may say "*hěn hǎohē* 很好喝", "very good to drink"; or "*bù hǎohē* 不好喝", "not good to drink".

For example：

● 中国茶很好喝。[Zhōngguó chá hěn hǎohē]
Chinese tea tastes good.

- 你的咖啡好喝吗？［Nǐ de kāfēi hǎohē ma］
Does your coffee taste good?
- 德国啤酒很好喝。［Déguó píjiě hěn hǎohē］
German beer tastes good.

Let's do some more exercises to review what we have learned today. Please try to translate them into Chinese.

- 中国人喜欢喝茶。
［Zhōngguó rén xǐhuan hē chá］
Chinese people like to drink tea.

- 我喜欢喝牛奶，不喜欢喝酸奶。
［Wǒ xǐhuan hē niúnǎi, bù xǐhuan hē suānnǎi］
I like to drink milk, but don't like yogurt.

- 青岛啤酒好喝吗？
［Qīngdǎo píjiǔ hǎohē ma］
Is Qingdao beer tasty?

- 对不起，我不喝酒。
［Duì bu qǐ, wǒ bù hē jiǔ］
I'm sorry, I don't drink wine.

Hope you got all of them correct. Download our app to access our lessons and exercises to help you review and test your comprehension. Remember, you can learn Chinese anywhere, anytime with **ChineseAny**.

Word List

Main Vocabulary		
喝［hē］ to drink	茶［chá］ tea	啤酒［píjiǔ］ wine，alcohol
酸奶［suān nǎi］ yogurt		
Additional Vocabulary		
好喝［hǎohē］ good to drink	酸［suān］ sour	酒［jiǔ］ wine，alcohol

Notes

① **好**［hǎo］ + **喝**［hē］ = **好喝**［hǎo hē］

e.g. ● 日本的茶也很好喝。［Rìběn de chá yě hěn hǎohē］
Japanese tea also tastes good.

● 咖啡不好喝。［Kāfēi bù hǎohē］
Coffee is not delicious.

● 中国的酸奶好喝吗？［Zhōngguó de suānnǎi hǎohē ma］
Does Chinese yogurt taste good?

Quiz

I. Pronunciation.

1. Please choose the initials or finals you heard.

1）A. shí　　　　　　　　B. sī

2) A. hóng   B. héng

3) A. zhōu   B. zhuō

4) A. zhǎo   B. jiào

2. **Please choose the Pinyin you heard.**

1) A. shǒujī   B. shǒuxù

2) A. wàimài   B. wàidài

3) A. diànshì   B. diànqì

4) A. fángjiān   B. fāngbiàn

II. **Form sentences.**

1. <u>wǒ</u>   <u>hěn</u>   <u>lǎoshī</u>   <u>lǎo</u>   <u>Hànyǔ</u>   <u>de</u>
    1   2   3   4   5   6

2. <u>Zhōngguó</u>   <u>hǎohē</u>   <u>de</u>   <u>ma</u>   <u>suānnǎi</u>
      1   2   3   4   5

3. <u>ma</u>   <u>jiǔ</u>   <u>ní</u>   <u>hē</u>
    1   2   3   4

4. <u>Zhōngguó</u>   <u>hěn</u>   <u>tāmen</u>   <u>xǐhuan</u>   <u>dōu</u>   <u>jiǔ</u>
      1   2   3   4   5   6

III. **Please translate the following sentences into Chinese.**

1. Do you like to drink Chinese tea?

2. They all like to drink beer.

3. I do not like to drink yogurt very much.

4. I am very busy ; I like to drink tea.

Do You Eat Breakfast

Welcome to Level One, Lesson Thirteen of **ChineseAny** podcast series teaching Chinese. Today we will learn four vocabularies, one verb and three nouns.

The 1st word is "*chī* 吃". "*chī* 吃" is a **verb**, it means "to eat". You may put **the food** after it.

> 吃
> [chī]
> to eat   verb

We have learned "*hǎohē* 好喝" in lesson twelve, so the same pattern can be used in "*hǎochī* 好吃", good to eat, it actually means "delicious, tasty".

OK, let's learn three nouns.

① The 1st one is "*mǐfàn* 米饭", it means "cooked rice". "*mǐ* 米" is "rice", "*fàn* 饭" means "meal".

> 米饭
> [mǐfàn]
> cooked rice

We have learned "*zǎo* 早" early; "*zhōngwǔ* 中午" noon; "*wǎn* 晚" late, before.

So breakfast in Chinese is "*zǎofàn* 早饭". We may say "*zhōngfàn* 中饭" or "*wǔfàn* 午饭" in Chinese, that's lunch. and dinner in Chinese is "*wǎnfàn 晚饭*".

② The 2nd one is "*miànbāo 面包*".
"*miànbāo 面包*" means "bread".
"*miàn 面*" means flour, noodles. "*bāo 包*" means bag.

面包
[miànbāo]
bread   noun

③ The 3rd one is "*dōngxi 东西*", it means something or object. "*dōng 东*" means east, "*xī 西*" means west.

There is one point that should be noted: the word "*xi 西*" in "*dōngxi 东西*" is pronounced in a neutral tone.

东西
[dōngxi]
object   noun

For example:
- 他不吃晚饭。[Tā bù chī zǎofàn]
  He doesn't eat dinner.
- 面包很好吃。[Miànbāo hěn hǎochī]
  The bread is very tasty.
- 中午我吃米饭。[Zhōngwǔ wǒ chī mǐfàn]
  I eat rice at noon.
- 你吃东西吗? [Nǐ chī dōngxi ma]
  Do you eat something?

Let's do some exercises to review what we have learned today. Please try to translate them into Chinese.

● 我是哈尔滨人，我喜欢吃米饭。

[Wǒ shì Hāěrbīn rén, wǒ xǐhuan chī mǐfàn]

I'm from Harbin; I like to eat rice.

● 我吃面包，谢谢。

[Wǒ chī miànbāo, xièxie]

I eat bread, thank you.

● 他很喜欢吃东西。

[Tā hěn xǐhuan chī dōngxi]

He is a good eater.

● 我的早饭很好吃。

[Wǒ de zǎofàn hěn hǎochī]

My breakfast is delicious.

● 我们都不吃晚饭。

[Wǒmen dōu bù chī wǎnfàn]

We all don't eat dinner.

● 你的先生吃早饭吗？

[Nǐ de xiānsheng chī zǎofàn ma]

Does your husband eat breakfast?

That wraps up today's lesson. Please do the exercises after class. Also, download our app to access our Chinese lessons. Remember, you can learn Chinese anywhere, anytime with **ChineseAny**.

◖ **Word List**

Main Vocabulary		
吃[chī] to eat	米饭[mǐfàn] rice	面包[miànbāo] bread
东西[dōngxi] thing/object		
Additional Vocabulary		
好吃[hǎochī] delicious	米[mǐ] rice	饭[fàn] meal
早饭[zǎofàn] breakfast	中饭[zhōngfàn] lunch	午饭[wǔfàn] lunch
晚饭[wǎnfàn] dinner	面[miàn] flour	包[bāo] bag
东[dōng] east	西[xī] west	

◖ **Notes**

① 好[hǎo] + 吃[chī] = 好吃[hǎo chī], **delicious**(**adj.**)

e. g. ● 中国饭很好吃。[Zhōngguó fàn hěn hǎochī]

    Chinese food is very delicious.

   ● 晚饭好吃吗？[Wǎnfàn hǎochī ma]

    Is the dinner delicious?

● 法国的面包很好吃。［Fǎguó miànbāo hěn hǎochī］
French bread is very delicious.

Quiz

I. Pronunciation.

1. Please choose the initials or finals you heard.

   1) A. jiǎn   B. juǎn

   2) A. mián   B. nián

   3) A. biàn   B. piàn

   4) A. kē   B. gē

2. Please choose the Pinyin you heard.

   1) A. yàoshì   B. yàoshi

   2) A. yìnxiàng   B. yǐngxiǎng

   3) A. táifēng   B. tāidòng

   4) A. hǎoxiàng   B. hǎo xiǎng

II. Form sentences.

1. mǐfàn   zǎofàn   xǐhuan   wǒ   chī
   1   2   3   4   5

   _____

2. Zhōngguó   hěn   fàn   hǎochī
   1   2   3   4

   _____

3. chī   nǐ   bù   ma   wǔfàn
   1   2   3   4   5

   _____

4. miàobāo   wǒ   xǐhuan   xiānsheng
   1   2   3   4

   _____

III. Please translate the following sentences into Chinese.

1. I like to eat rice；my husband likes to eat bread.

   _____

2. They are all very tired.

   _____

3. My Chinese teacher eats rice for dinner.

   _____

4. I like your bag very much.

   _____

Watch Movie

Welcome to Level One, Lesson Fourteen of **ChineseAny** podcast series teaching Chinese. Today we will learn three new characters, and one pattern.

The 1st word is "*kàn* 看". "*kàn* 看" is a **verb** which means to look or to watch.

看
[kàn]
to see, watch   verb

We may put **a verb** after "*hǎo* 好", which we have learned before, so "*hǎokàn* 好看" can also be translated to "pretty" or "beautiful", and it is an **adjective**. You may say "*hěn hǎokàn* 很好看", very good-looking; or "*bù hǎokàn* 不好看", not good-looking.

OK, let's see our two nouns.
① The 1st one is "*diànyǐng* 电影". "*diànyǐng* 电影" means "movie". So the phrase "watch movie" should be "*kàn diànyǐng* 看电影".

电影
[diànyǐng]
movie   noun

For example：
- 他喜欢看电影。[Tā xǐhuan kàn diànyǐng]
  He likes to watch movies.
- 他喜欢看美国电影。[Tā xǐhuan kàn Měiguó diànyǐng]

He likes to watch American movies.

② The 2nd word is "*jīntiān* 今天". It
means "today".

It's a phrase about time. We have
learned how to say morning,
afternoon and evening in Chinese

今天
[jīntiān]
today   noun

in Lesson 5, so you may say "this morning", "*jīntiān zǎoshang*
今天早上"; "this evening", "*jīntiān wǎnshang* 今天晚上".

The basic Chinese sentence is composed of：

Subject ＋ Time phrase ＋ Location ＋ Verb ＋ Object

You may also put **THE TIME PHRASE** before the Subject for emphasis.

Time phrase ＋ **Subject** ＋ Location ＋ Verb ＋ Object

For example：

● 我们今天看中国电影。[Wǒmen jīntiān kàn Zhōngguó diànyǐng]
We will watch a Chinese movie today.

● 他今天早饭吃面包。[Tā jīntiān zǎofàn chī miànbāo]
He eats bread for breakfast today.

● 我今天不喝啤酒。[Wǒ Jīntiān bù hē píjiǔ]
I don't drink beer today.

Also you may put "*Jīntiān* 今天" before the subject in the three
sentences above to emphasize "**today**".

Let's do some exercises to review what we have known so far.
Please try to translate them into Chinese.

● 今天晚上我见我的老师?
[Jīntiān wǎnshang wǒ jiàn wǒ de lǎoshī]
This evening I (will) meet my teacher.

● 他的电影很好看。
[Tā de diànyǐng hěn hǎokàn]
His movie is very good.

● 今天的早饭好吃吗?
[Jīntiān de zǎofàn hǎochī ma]
Is today's breakfast delicious?

● 我不喜欢看电影,你呢?
[Wǒ bù xǐhuan kàn diànyǐng, nǐ ne]
I don't like watching movies, and you?

Great, that wraps up today's lesson, please do the exercises after the class or download our app to access our Chinese lessons. Remember you can learn Chinese anywhere, anytime with *ChineseAny*.

◗ **Word List**

Main Vocabulary		
看[kàn] to see, to watch	电影[diànyǐng] movie	今天[jīntiān] today
Additional Vocabulary		
好看[hǎokàn] pretty, beautiful		

Notes

① 好[hǎo] + 看[kàn] = 好看[hǎo kàn] good-looking (adj.)

  e. g. ● 他的太太很好看。[Tā de tàitai hěn hǎokàn]

       His wife is very perrty.

      ● 电影好看吗? [Tā de diànyǐng bù hǎokà]

       Is the movie good?

② **Subject + Time phrase + Location + Verb + Object** or
Time phrase + Subject + Location + Verb + Object

  e. g. ● 今天我们都喝中国茶。[Jīntiān wǒmen dōu hē Zhōngguó chá]

      We all drink Chinese tea today.

      ● 今天他们也看美国电影。[Jīntiān tāmen yě kàn Měiguó diànyǐng]

       They also watch American movies today.

Quiz

I. Pronunciation.

  1. Please choose the initials or finals you heard.

    1) A. bài   B. pài

    2) A. liǎn   B. niǎn

    3) A. chí   B. cí

    4) A. wǒ   B. wǔ

  2. Please choose the Pinyin you heard.

    1) A. diànyǐng   B. diànyīn

2) A. kànjiàn   B. kàndào

3) A. gànjìn   B. gānjìng

4) A. diàntī   B. jīntiān

II. Form sentences.

1. diànyǐng   wǒmen   kàn   jīntiān   Zhōngguó

    1   2   3   4   5

2. zǎofàn   zǎoshang   bù   wǒ   jīntiān   chī

    1   2   3   4   5   6

3. wǒ   kàn   bù   xǐhuan   xiānsheng   diànyǐng

    1   2   3   4   5   6

4. hěn   jīntiān   dōu   wǒmen   lèi

    1   2   3   4   5

III. Please translate the following sentences into Chinese.

1. Today's movie is very nice.

2. We are also very tired today.

3. Today I will meet my Chinese teacher.

4. Do you like to watch Chinese movies?

Listen to the Music

Welcome to Level One, Lesson Fifteen of our **ChineseAny** podcast series teaching Mandarin Chinese. Today we will learn three new words. They are:

The 1st word, "*tīng* 听".

"*tīng* 听", to listen.

The 2nd word, "*yīnyuè* 音乐".

"*yīnyuè* 音乐", music.

The 3rd word, "*míngtiān* 明天".

"*míngtiān* 明天", tomorrow.

听	[tīng]	to listen	verb
音乐	[yīnyuè]	music	noun
明天	[míngtiān]	tomorrow	noun

OK, let's do some exercises to practice what we have learned so far.

- listen to music: *tīng yīnyuè* 听音乐
- like listening to music: *xǐhuan tīng yīnyuè* 喜欢听音乐
- Chinese music: *Zhōngguó yīnyuè* 中国音乐
- good music: *hǎotīng de yīnyuè* 好听的音乐

Great, let's try to make some sentences:

- 我喜欢听音乐。[Wǒ xǐhuan tīng yīnyuè]
  I like listening to music.
- 明天我们听中国音乐。[Míngtiān wǒmen tīng Zhōngguó yīnyuè]
  Tomorrow we shall listen to Chinese music.
- 你喜欢他们的音乐吗? [Nǐ xǐhuan tāmen de yīnyuè ma]

Do you like their music?

- 他们也不喜欢听音乐。[Tāmen yě bù xǐhuan tīng yīnyuè]

  They don't like listening to music either.

- 明天晚上他们都不听音乐。[Míngtiān wǎnshang tāmen dōu bù tīng yīnyuè]

  Tomorrow evening，none of them will listen to the music.

In our lessons，we have learned：

"*hǎo chī 好吃*" delicious.

"*hǎo hē 好喝*" good to drink.

"*hǎo kàn 好看*" good-looking. (depending on the context)

So today we will add another one "*hǎo tīng 好听*"，which means being pleasant to listen to.

You may say

- 他的音乐很好听。[Tā de yīnyuè hěn hǎotīng]

  His music is nice/good.

- 他的音乐不好听。[Tā de yīnyuè bù hǎotīng]

  His music is not nice/good.

That wraps up today's lesson. Please do the exercises after class. Also，download our app to access our Chinese lessons. Remember，you can learn Chinese anywhere，anytime with **ChineseAny**.

◖ **Word List**

Main Vocabulary		
听[tīng] to listen to, hear	音乐[yīnyuè] music	明天[míngtiān] tomorrow

Additional Vocabulary
好听 [hǎotīng]
nice

Notes

① 好 [hǎo] **+** 吃 [chī] / 喝 [hē] / 看 [kàn] / 听 [tīng]

很 [hěn] / 不 [bù] **+** 好吃 [hǎochī] / 好喝 [hǎohē] / 好看 [hǎokàn] / 好听 [hǎotīng]

e. g. ● 她的音乐不好听。[Tā de yīnyuè bù hǎotīng]

Her music isn't good.

● 中国饭很好吃。[Zhōngguó fàn hěn hǎochī]

Chinese food is very delicious.

● 中国茶好喝吗？[Zhōngguó chá hǎohē ma]

Is Chinese tea delicious?

● 咖啡不好喝。[Kāfēi bù hǎohē]

Coffee does not taste good.

Quiz

I. Pronunciation.

1. Please choose the initials or finals you heard.

1) A. zài   B. zàn

2) A. bāo   B. gāo

3) A. wǒ   B. guǒ

4) A. jīn   B. jīng

2. Please choose the Pinyin you heard.

1) A. yīnyuè　　　　　B. yīngyǔ

2) A. míngtiān　　　　B. míngnián

3) A. hǎo huài　　　　B. hǎo guài

4) A. tīngshuō　　　　B. tíngchē

II. Form sentences.

1. míngtiān　　miànbāo　　zǎoshang　　chī　　wǒ
　　　1　　　　　2　　　　　　3　　　　　4　　　5

_____

2. Zhōngguó　　hěn　　yīnyuè　　hǎotīng
　　　1　　　　2　　　3　　　　4

_____

3. máng　　jīntiān　　bù　　wǎnshang　　wǒ
　　1　　　2　　　3　　　4　　　　5

_____

4. yīnyuè　　xǐhuan　　tāmen　　dōu　　yě　　hěn
　　1　　　2　　　3　　　4　　5　　6

_____

III. Please translate the following sentences into Chinese.

1. Tomorrow morning I am not busy; tomorrow evening I am very busy.

_____

2. My wife likes to listen to Chinese music.

_____

3. She does not eat dinner.

_____

4. See you tomorrow, Teacher Sophie.

_____

This and That

Welcome to Level One, Lesson Sixteen of our **ChineseAny** podcast series teaching Mandarin Chinese. Today we will learn three new vocabulary words, two pronouns and one measure word.

Let's look at them now.

The two pronouns:

The 1st one:

"*zhè* 这", in the 4th tone, this.

这
[zhè]
This   pronoun

The 2nd one:

"*nà* 那", in the 4th tone, that.

"this is" "*zhè shì* 这是".

"that is" "*nà shì* 那是".

那
[nà]
That   pronoun

For example:

- 这是我的太太。[Zhè shì wǒ de tàitai]
  This is my wife.

- 这不是我的学生。[Zhè bú shì wǒ de xuésheng]
  This is not my student.

- 这是你的汉语老师吗?[Zhè shì nǐ de Hànyǔ lǎoshī ma]
  Is this your Chinese teacher?

- 那是他的妈妈。[Nà shì tā de māma]
  That is his Mom.

● 那不是她的咖啡。［Nà bú shì tā de kāfēi］

That is not her coffee.

那是你的早饭吗？［Nà shì nǐ de zǎofàn ma］

Is that your breakfast?

OK, let's look at the 3rd vocabulary,
which is a measure word "gè 个".

There are about one hundred different
measure words in Chinese.

个
［gè］
Counting word

We always use the measure words before the nouns and different
nouns should use different measure words. "gè 个" is the most common
one. So before you learn other measure words, you may use "gè 个".

So "this one" in Chinese is "zhè ge
这个"; "gè 个" usually changes to the
neutral tone.

这［zhè］
那［nà］ } 个［gè］ + Noun

This movie, "zhè ge diànyǐng 这个电
影"; that person, "nàge rén 那个人".

OK, let's do some translation exercises.

● 我喜欢看这个电影，你呢？［Wǒ xǐhuan kàn zhège diànyǐng, nǐ ne］
   I like to watch this movie, and you?

● 这个咖啡好喝吗？［Zhè ge kāfēi hǎohē ma］
   Is this coffee good?

● 那个老师很好看。［Nà ge lǎshī hěn hǎokàn］
   That teacher is very pretty.

● 这是我们汉语老师的茶。［Zhè shì wǒmen Hànyǔ lǎoshī de chá］
   This is our Chinese teacher's tea.

● 这是今天的晚饭。［Zhè shì jīntiān de wǎnfàn］
   This is today's dinner.

This is our lesson for today. Hope you have learned something here. Please do the exercises to review and test your comprehension. Download our app to access our Chinese lessons. Remember, you can learn Chinese anywhere, anytime with **ChineseAny**.

Word List

Main Vocabulary		
这 [zhè] this	那 [nà] that	个 [gè] measure word

Notes

这个 [zhè ge]/**那个** [nà ge] **+ 是** [shì] **+ noun**：

e.g. ● 这是我的儿子。[Zhè shì wǒ de érzi]

This is my son.

● 那是她的水。[Nà shì tā de shuǐ]

That is her water.

● 这不是啤酒。[Zhè bú shì píjiǔ]

This is not bear.

Quiz

I. Pronunciation.

1. Please choose the initials or finals you heard.

1) A. guān   B. guāng

2) A. wài   B. hài

3) A. jiǎn   B. jiǎo

4) A. nèn   B. nèi

2. Please choose the Pinyin you heard.

1) A. shàngge   B. shàngkè

2) A. nà ge   B. nǎ ge

3) A. gēge   B. gègè

4) A. qìchuǎn   B. qǐchuáng

II. Form sentences.

1. <u>hǎokàn</u>   <u>zhège</u>   <u>hěn</u>   <u>diànyǐng</u>
   1   2   3   4

_____

2. <u>hē</u>   <u>wǒ</u>   <u>zhège</u>   <u>xǐhuan</u>
 1   2   3   4

_____

3. <u>zhège</u>   <u>hǎo</u>   <u>rén</u>   <u>Hànyǔ</u>   <u>de</u>   <u>hěn</u>
   1   2   3   4   5   6

_____

4. <u>nǐ</u>   <u>bāo</u>   <u>xǐhuan</u>   <u>ma</u>   <u>zhège</u>
 1   2   3   4   5

_____

III. Please translate the following sentences into Chinese.

1. I like to watch this Chinese movie.

_____

2. Do you like that Chinese teacher?

_____

3. They all eat bread.

_____

4. This is Sophie, and she is a Chinese teacher.

_____

I Have a Little Milk

Welcome to Level One, Lesson Seventeen of our **ChineseAny** podcast series teaching Chinese. Today we will learn three new vocabulary words, two verbs and one quantifier.

The 1st verb is "*yǒu* 有", means "have, has or there is". To say "I have . . ." in Chinese is "*wǒ yǒu* . . . "

有
[yǒu]
have/has   verb

Sentence Pattern：
Somebody + *yǒu* 有 + something.

For example：

- 我有水。[Wǒ yǒu shuǐ]
  I have water.
- 他有汉语老师。[Tā yǒu Hànyǔ lǎoshī]
  He has a Chinese teacher.

Sb. + 有 + something
   [yǒu]
sb. have/has something

For questions, to ask "do you have . . . ?" in Chinese is "*nǐ yǒu* . . . *ma* 你有……吗？"

Sb. + 有 + Sth. + 吗？
   [yǒu]   [ma]
Do you have . . . ?

For the opposite of "have", you **CANNOT** say "*bù yǒu* 不有", but "*méiyǒu* 没有", which means "don't have, didn't have or will not have".

The 2nd verb is "*shuō* 说", to say or to speak.

Normally we use the content behind "*shuō* 说", rather than put subject pronouns after it.

说
[shuō]
to say   verb

For example：

- 我说汉语。[Wǒ shuō Hànyǔ]

  I speak Chinese.

- 你说英语吗? [Nǐ shuō Yīngyǔ ma]

  Do you speak English?

The 3rd vocabulary word is a quantifier, "*yìdiǎnr* 一点儿" a little bit, a few or some.

Normally we put a **noun** after it, like "some beer", "*yìdiǎn píjiǔ* 一点儿啤酒", "a few things", "*yìdiǎn dōngxi* 一点儿东西".

一点儿
[yìdiǎnr]
a little   quantifier

For example：

- 我说一点儿汉语。[Wǒ shuō yìdiǎnr Hànyǔ]

  I speak a little Chinese.

- 他没有午饭。[Tā méiyǒu wǔfàn]

  She has no lunch.

- 我们没有咖啡,对不起。[Wǒmen méiyǒu kāfēi, duì bu qǐ]

  We don't have coffee, sorry.

- 我有水,你喝吗? [Wǒ yǒu shuǐ, nǐ hē ma]

  I have some water, do you want to drink?

Now let's try to learn something else.

We learned "*yǒu* 有" and we learned "*yìdiǎnr* 一点儿".

If we put them together, "*yǒu yìdiǎnr* 有一点儿", It means to be/have a little bit. We need to put an adjective after it when you are not very happy or satisfied with somebody or something.

> 有 + (一) 点儿 + adj.
> [yǒu] [yìdiǎnr]
> a little + adjective

For example：

- 有点儿累 [yǒu diǎnr lèi]
  a little bit tired
- 有点儿忙 [yǒu diǎnr máng]
  a little bit busy
- 有点儿不高兴 [yǒu diǎnr bù gāoxìng]
  a little bit upset
- 有点儿晚 [yǒu diǎnr wǎn]
  a little bit late

This is our lesson for today. Hope you have learned something. Please do the exercises to review and test your comprehension. Download our app to access our Chinese lessons. Remember, you can learn Chinese anywhere, anytime with **ChineseAny**.

Word List

Main Vocabulary		
有 [yǒu] to have	说 [shuō] to say, speak	一点儿 [yìdiǎnr] a little bit
Additional Vocabulary		
有点儿 [yǒu diǎnr] a little	没有 [méi yǒu] do not have	

Notes

① **Sb.** + (没[méi]) **有**[yǒu] + **sth.**

  e. g. ● 他有中国电影。[Tā yǒu Zhōngguó diànyǐng]

         He has Chinese movies.

       ● 我没有咖啡。[Wǒ méi yǒu kāfēi]

         I don't have coffee.

       ● 他没有老师。[Tā méi yǒu lǎoshī]

         He does not have a teacher.

② **Verb** + **一点儿**[yì diǎnr] + **noun**

  e. g. ● 我有一点儿啤酒。[Wǒ yǒu yìdiǎnr píjiǔ]

         I have a little beer.

       ● 喝一点儿东西。[Hē yìdiǎnr dōngxi]

         Drink something.

       ● 我们晚上喝一点酸奶。[Wǒmen wǎnshang hē yìdiǎn suānnǎi]

         We drink some yogurt in the evening.

③ **有**[yǒu] + **一点儿**[yìdiǎnr] + **adj.**

  e. g. ● 他有点儿不高兴。[Tā yǒu diǎnr bù gāoxìng]

         He is a little sad.

       ● 你有点儿晚。[Nǐ yǒu diǎnr wǎn]

         You are a little late.

       ● 咖啡有点儿不好喝。[Kāfēi yǒu diǎnr bù hǎohē]

         Coffee is a little terrible.

Quiz

I. Pronunciation.

  1. Please choose the initials or finals you heard.

1) A. niú   B. liú
2) A. zǎi   B. zǎo
3) A. shī   B. sī
4) A. jì   B. xì

2. Please choose the Pinyin you heard.

1) A. yìdiǎn   B. yídiǎn
2) A. yǒuwú   B. yǒuwù
3) A. tǐnghǎo   B. tīnghǎo
4) A. yánzhòng   B. yǎnzhōng

II. Form sentences.

1. wǒmen   lǎoshī   méi   yě   yǒu   Hànyǔ
     1   2   3   4   5   6

2. máng   jīntiān   yǒu   zǎoshang   yìdiǎn
     1   2   3   4   5

3. Hànyǔ   shuō   tā   xǐhuan
     1   2   3   4

4. wǒ   tīng   tā   bù   kāfēi   shuō   hē
     1   2   3   4   5   6   7

III. Please translate the following sentences into Chinese.

1. I am a little hungry, and you?

2. I have a little milk, do you drink it?

3. I heard that your Chinese teacher did not like to drink coffee.

4. Sorry, we do not have that movie.

I Want to . . .

Welcome to Level One, Lesson Eighteen of our **ChineseAny** podcast series teaching Mandarin Chinese. Today we will learn three new vocabulary words, one helping word and two verbs. Let's see them now.

The 1st word is a helping word "*kěyǐ* 可以". Two charcters in this word are both in the 3rd tone. The first 3rd tone should be changed to the 2nd tone.

可以
[kěyǐ]
May, could   helping word

"*kěyǐ* 可以", may, could. We always put it before the **verb**, which means "you may, you could, or you can do something".

For example,
- 我可以说汉语。[Wǒ kěyǐ shuō Hànyǔ]
  I can speak Chinese.
- 我可以喝这个吗? [Wǒ kěyǐ hē zhège ma]
  Can I drink this?

But if you use the negative form, "*bù kěyǐ* 不可以", the meaning is "cannot/not allowed to do something."

不 + 可以 + Verb
[bù] [kěyǐ]
Cannot/not allowed to do something

91

For example，

- 你不可以喝啤酒。[Nǐ bù kěyǐ hē píjiǔ]
  You cannot drink beer.

The 2nd vocabulary is a verb "*mǎi*
买"，to buy，to purchase. You may put
the noun after it to express what to buy.
For example：

- 买东西 [mǎi dōngxi]
  to purchase something
- 买牛奶 [mǎi niúnǎi]
  to buy milk

| 买 |
| [mǎi] |
| to buy verb |

The 3rd vocabulary is a verb "*xiǎng*
想"，In Chinese "*xiǎng 想*" has 3
common meanings.

The 1st meaning is "want to do
something". Normally we put a verb after it.
For example：

- 我想喝水。[Wǒ xiǎng hē shuǐ]
  I want to drink water.
- 我想听音乐。[Wǒ xiǎng tīng yīnyuè]
  I want to listen to music.

| 想 |
| [xiǎng] |
| to think/miss/want verb |

The 2nd meaning is to miss somebody，something or someplace.
You may also use it to say "I miss somebody very much".
For example：

- 我很想我的太太。[Wǒ hěn xiǎng wǒ de tàitai]
  I miss my wife very much.

- 我想你。[Wǒ xiǎng nǐ]

   I miss you.

The 3rd meaning is "to think or in one's opinion".

For example：

- 我想你不是中国人。[Wǒ xiǎng nǐ bú shì Zhōngguó rén]

   I think you are not Chinese.

- 我想她很忙。[Wǒ xiǎng tā hěn máng]

   I think she is busy.

Great，let's do some exercises to practice what we have learned today.

- 明天我想买东西。

   [Míngtiān wǒ xiǎng mǎi dōngxi]

   Tomorrow I shall want to purchase something.

- 我可以看这个电影吗?

   [Wǒ kěyǐ kàn zhège diànyǐng ma]

   Can I see this movie?

- 我买这个，谢谢。

   [Wǒ mǎi zhè ge, xièxie]

   I will buy this, thank you.

- 我可以说一点儿英语。

   [Wǒ kěyǐ shuō yìdiǎn Yīngyǔ]

   I may speak a little English.

   This is today's lesson. This is the last lesson of Elementary Level One. Now that you have completed this level，please be sure to check out our practice library to test what you have learned in this level. Please do the exercises to review and test your comprehension. Download our app to access our Chinese lesson. Remember，you can learn Chinese anywhere，anytime with **ChineseAny**.

Word List

Main Vocabulary		
可以[kěyǐ] can	买[mǎi] to buy	想[xiǎng] to want, think, miss

Notes

① 可以[kěyǐ] + verb：

Statement sentence：subject + 可以[kěyǐ] + verb + object.

Negative sentence：subject + 不[bù] + 可以[kěyǐ] + verb + object.

e.g. ● 我太太可以说汉语。[Wǒ tàitai kěyǐ shuō Hànyǔ]

My wife can speak Chinese.

● 你晚上不可以喝咖啡。[Nǐ wǎnshang bù kěyǐ hē kāfēi]

You cannot drink coffee at night.

● 明天早上我不可以吃早饭。[Míngtiān zǎoshang wǒ bù kěyǐ chī zǎofàn]

I cannot eat breakfast tomorrow morning.

② 想[xiǎng]：

To want to do

● 我想喝茶。[Wǒ xiǎng hē chā]

I want to drink tea.

● 他想喝酸奶。[Tā xiǎng hē suānnǎi]

He wants to drink yogurt.

To miss

● 我很想你。[Wǒ hěn xiǎng nǐ]

I miss you very much.

● 他想他的太太。[Tā xiǎng tā de tàitai]

He misses his wife.

To think

● 我想他是英语老师。[Wǒ xiǎng tā shì Yīngyǔ lǎoshī]

I think he is an English teacher.

● 我想他们的关系很好。[Wǒ xiǎng tāmen de guānxi hěn hǎo]

I think their relationship is very good.

Quiz

I. Pronunciation.

1. Please choose the initials or finals you heard.

1) A. lǐ　　　　　　　　B. nǐ

2) A. biàn　　　　　　　B. piàn

3) A. qī　　　　　　　　B. xī

4) A. léi　　　　　　　　B. nèi

2. Please choose the Pinyin you heard.

1) A. kěyǐ　　　　　　　B. kèqi

2) A. xiāngxìn　　　　　B. xiángxì

3) A. miánhuā　　　　　B. miǎnhuái

4) A. shǒujī　　　　　　B. shǒuxù

II. Form sentences.

1. <u>ma</u>　<u>nǐ</u>　<u>shuō</u>　<u>kěyǐ</u>　<u>Hànyǔ</u>
　　1　　2　　3　　　4　　　5

2. <u>zhè ge</u>   <u>xiǎng</u>   <u>dōngxi</u>   <u>wǒ</u>   <u>mǎi</u>
   1   2   3   4   5

3. <u>wǒ</u>   <u>diànyǐng</u>   <u>xiǎng</u>   <u>nà ge</u>   <u>kàn</u>
   1   2   3   4   5

4. <u>nǐ</u> <u>bù</u> <u>zhè ge</u> <u>kěyǐ</u> <u>mǎi</u>
   1   2   3   4   5

III. Please translate the following sentences into Chinese.

1. Can you speak a little Chinese?

2. I think he does not like me.

3. I miss China, and I miss my Chinese teacher.

4. This bread is very delicious. Do you want to buy?

二

级

What's Your Name

Welcome to Elementary Level Two, Lesson One of our **ChineseAny** podcast series teaching Mandarin Chinese. Starting today, we will begin our Level Two Lesson. Today we will learn three words, one special question word, one verb, and one noun. "Special questions are those questions that ask for details. They are also called Wh-questions as most of them start with 'wh'." For example: "What? Which? When? Where? Why? Whose?"

Let's look at them now. The 1st one, "*shénme* 什么", what.

> 什么
> [shénme]
> what   interrogative word

In Chinese, we always use it as a noun or put it before a noun to make a special question, Please pay attention to this point, in special questions, we **CANNOT** use "*ma* 吗".

> 什么 + noun
> [shénme]
> what + noun?
> special question

Remember, we can **ONLY** use "*ma* 吗" in yes-no questions.

> ... ma 吗?
> "yes-no" questions

For example：

- 你吃什么？［Nǐ chī shénme］
  What do you eat?

- 你的先生喝什么？［Nǐ de xiānshēng hē shénme］
  What does your husband drink?

- 这是什么？［Zhè shì shénme］
  What is this?

- 你喜欢喝什么茶？［Nǐ xǐhuān hē shénme chá］
  What tea do you like to drink?

- 你想看什么电影？［Nǐ xiǎng kàn shénme diànyǐng］
  What movie would you like to watch?

OK，now let's see the 2nd word, "*jiào* 叫".

It is a verb which means "to call or to be called". We may use that to introduce your full name.

> Sb. + 叫 + full name
> ［jiào］
> introduce your full name

For example：

- 我叫玛姬。［Wǒ jiào Maggie］
  I'm called Maggie or please call me Maggie.

- 你叫什么？［Nǐ jiào shénme］
  What's your name?

OK，the last word, "*míngzì* 名字", name.

Your name, "*nǐ de míngzì* 你的名字", My name "*wǒ de míngzì* 我的名字".

> 名字
> ［míngzì］
> **Name noun**

For example：

- 你叫什么名字? ［Nǐ jiào shénme míngzì］

  What's your name?

- 你的名字很好听。［Nǐ de míngzì hěn hǎotīng］

  Your name is nice.

Here let's learn something else.

The "*míng* 名" in "*míngzì* 名字" means name. The "*zì* 字" means character.

Previously，we have learned that Chinese language is "*Hànyǔ* 汉语"，so "*Hànzì* 汉字" means Chinese character.

汉语 ⟹	汉字
［*Hànyǔ*］	［*Hànzì*］

OK，please try to translate and read the following examples，based on what we have learned today.

- 我们今天吃什么饭?

  ［Wǒmen jīntiān chī shénme fàn］

  What shall we eat today?

- 你想喝什么咖啡?

  ［Nǐ xiǎng hē shénme kāfēi］

  What coffee do you like to drink?

- 这个不是汉字.

  ［Zhège bú shì hànzì］

  This is not the Chinese character.

- 中国的汉字很好看。

  ［Zhōngguó de hànzì hěn hǎokàn］

  Chinese character is nice.

Great，so that wraps up today's lesson. Hope you learned something. Download our app to access our Chinese lessons，Remember，you can learn Chinese anywhere，anytime with **ChineseAny**.

○ **Word List**

Main Vocabulary		
什么[shénme] what	叫[jiào] to call, to be known as	名字[míngzi] name
Additional Vocabulary		
字[zì] character, word	汉字[Hànzì] Chinese character	

○ **Notes**

Wh-question sentences

Subject + verb + 什么[shénme] + object

e. g. ● 你叫什么名字? [Nǐ jiào shénme míngzi]

What's your name?

● 你想看什么电影? [Nǐ xiǎng kàn shénme diànyǐng]

What movie would you like to watch?

○ **Quiz**

I. Pronunciation.

1. Please choose the initials or finals you heard.

1) A. zǎo   B. zhǎo

2) A. kài   B. kuài

3) A. nán   B. nián

4) A. hǎo   B. kǎo

2. Please choose the Pinyin you heard.

1) A. shénme   B. zěnme

2) A. jiǎozi   B. jiàozi

3) A. míngzi   B. miànzi

4) A. zhīdào   B. zhìzào

II. Form sentences.

1. <u>kàn</u>   <u>nǐ</u>   <u>diànyǐng</u>   <u>xǐhuan</u>   <u>shénme</u>
    1   2   3   4   5

2. <u>shénme</u>   <u>jiào</u>   <u>míngzi</u>   <u>nǐ</u>
    1   2   3   4

3. <u>chī</u>   <u>jīntiān</u>   <u>shénme</u>   <u>wǒmen</u>
    1   2   3   4

4. <u>hē</u>   <u>nǐ</u>   <u>shénme</u>   <u>zǎoshang</u>
    1   2   3   4

III. Please translate the following sentences into Chinese.

1. What is this?

2. What would you like to eat?

3. What music do you want to listen to?

4. What do you want to buy tomorrow?

I Want . . .

Welcome to Elementary Level Two, Lesson Two of our *ChineseAny* podcast series teaching Chinese. Today we will learn three new words, one helping word and two verbs.

Let's look at them now.

The 1st one, "*yào* 要", "*yào* 要" means want something or want to do something.

> 要
> [yào]
> want   helping word

You may put a noun after it to express what you want

> 要 + noun
> [yào]   want something

or put a verb after it to express the intention to do something.

> 要 + verb
> [yào]
> want to do something

For example：

● A：你要什么? [Nǐ yào shénme?]

What do you want?

- B：我要这个。［wǒ yào Zhège］

    I want this.

- 我不要咖啡，谢谢！［wǒ bú yào kāfēi，xièxie！］

  I don't want coffee，thank you！

Let's move to our 2nd vocabulary，
"*xuéxí 学习*"．"*xuéxí 学习*" means "to
study，to learn"．

学习
［xuéxí］
to study   verb

For example：

- 学习汉语［xuéxí hànyǔ］

  study Chinese

- 学习英语［xuéxí yīngyǔ］

  study English

- 学习什么［xuéxí shénme］

  study what

- 你要学习什么?［Nǐ yào xuéxí shénme］

  What do you want to study?

Normally，you may use "*xué 学*" alone.

OK，the last word，"*zuò 做*"，to
make，to do.

Usually we use it to express that you
make or do something with your hands.

做
［zuò］
to make，to do   verb

For example：

- 做什么?［zuò shénme］

  to do what?

- 你喜欢做什么?［Nǐ xǐhuān zuò shénme］

What do you like to do?

● 你要做什么？［Nǐ yào zuò shénme］

What do you want to do?

Now let's learn something else.

In Level one, we have learned how to say "meal, food" in Chinese, that is "fàn 饭". So "to make food" in Chinese is "zuòfàn 做饭".

The last thing we need to learn is the difference between "xiǎng 想" and "yào 要".

● "xiǎng 想", has three meanings："would like, think or miss." Let's see the patterns.

想［xiǎng］：

+ verb — would like, want(soft)

+ sentence — to think ...

+ somebody — to miss ...

  ● ~ + verb：would like, want

  ● ~ + sentence：to think

  ● ~ + somebody：to miss

  ● "yào 要"：

followed by VERB or NOUN, means "want", which is stronger than " xiǎng 想". Let's see the patterns.

要［yào］：

+ verb — want to do sth(strong)

+ noun — want sth

  ● ~ + verb：want to do sth.

  ● ~ + noun：want sth.

For the negative form，"bù xiǎng 不想" means "wouldn't like or don't want to do something". But "bú yào 不要" is very strong, which means "forbidding or not allowing one to do something".

OK，please try to translate and read the examples，which will help us review what we have learned today.

- 我想中国人不喜欢喝咖啡。
  [Wǒ xiǎng Zhōngguó rén bù xǐhuān hē kāfēi]
  I think Chinese people don't like drinking coffee.

- 我今天不想学习。
  [Wǒ jīntiān bù xiǎng xuéxí]
  I don't want to study today.

- 今天晚上你可以做饭吗?
  [Jīntiān wǎnshàng nǐ kěyǐ zuòfàn ma]
  Can you cook tonight?

- 你不要喝牛奶!
  [Nǐ búyào hē niúnǎi]
  Don't drink milk!

Great，so that wraps up today's lesson. Hope you have learned something. Download our app to access our Chinese lessons. Remember you can learn Chinese anywhere，anytime with **ChineseAny**.

⬤ Word List

Main Vocabulary		
要[yào] to want	学习[xuéxí] to study	做[zuò] to do；to make

Additional Vocabulary		
学[xué] to study；to learn	做饭[zuòfàn] to cook；prepare a meal	

Notes

Modal verbs "想"[xiǎng] **and "要"**[yào]

➤ **想**(xiǎng) { **+ verb — to want to do something**(soft)
+ sentence — to think
+ somebody — to miss }

e.g. ● 你想吃什么？[Nǐ xiǎng chī shénme?]（want）

What do you want to eat?

● 我想学汉字。[wǒ xiǎng xué Hànzì]（want）

I want to learn Chinese characters.

● 我想中国人不喜欢喝咖啡。[Wǒ xiǎng Zhōngguó rén bù xǐhuan hē kāfēi]（think）

I think the Chinese don't like coffee.

● 我很想你，你呢？[Wǒ hěn xiǎng nǐ, nǐ ne]（miss）

I miss you very much, and you?

➤ **要**(yào) { **+ verb — to want to do something**(strong)
+ noun — to want something }

e.g. ● 你要学习什么？[Nǐ yào xuéxí shénme]

What do you want to study?

● 你要做什么？[Nǐ yào zuò shénme]

What do you want to do?

Quiz

I. Pronunciation.

1. Please choose the initials or finals you heard.

   1) A. kòu　　　　　　　　B. kuò

   2) A. hóng　　　　　　　B. héng

   3) A. zhuāng　　　　　　B. zuān

   4) A. wèn　　　　　　　 B. wèi

2. Please choose the Pinyin you heard.

   1) A. xūyào　　　　　　　B. jiùyào

   2) A. xuéxí　　　　　　　B. xuéjí

   3) A. shūkān　　　　　　B. shùgàn

   4) A. zīliào　　　　　　　B. jīyào

II. Form sentences.

1. nǐ　　shénme　　yào
   　1　　　2　　　　3

   _____

2. fàn　　jīntiān　　shénme　　nǐ　　zuò
   　1　　　2　　　　　3　　　　4　　5

   _____

3. wǒ　　Hànyǔ　　míngtiān　　xuéxí　　zǎoshang
   　1　　　2　　　　3　　　　　4　　　　5

   _____

4. hē　　wǒ　　kāfēi　　xiǎng
   　1　　　2　　　3　　　4

   _____

III. Please translate the following sentences into Chinese.

1. What do you like to do?

_____

2. What do you want to study?

_____

3. Do you cook?

_____

4. What character do you want to study?

_____

What Is Your Family Name

Welcome to Elementary Level Two, Lesson Three of our **ChineseAny** podcast series teaching Chinese. Today we will learn three vocabularies, two nouns and one adjective.

Let's look at them now.

The 1st one, "*xìng* 姓", family name.

姓
[xìng]
family name   noun

It can be used as a noun or a verb, you may say "*Somebody + xìng* 姓 *+ family name*" to introduce your name.

sb. + 姓 + family
[xìng]
name verb

So you may introduce

- 我姓马,我叫马云。[Wǒ xìng Mǎ, wǒ jiào Mǎyún]
  My family name is Ma; My full name is Yun Ma.

- 你姓什么? [Nǐ xìng shénme]
  What's your family name?

- 你叫什么? [Nǐ jiào shénme]
  What's your full name?

OK, the 2nd word is "*péngyǒu* 朋友", friend.

朋友
[péngyǒu]
friend   noun

For example：

- 好朋友 ［hǎo péngyǒu］
  Good friend
- 你是我的好朋友。［Nǐ shì wǒde hǎo péngyǒu］
  You are my good friend.

OK, the 3rd word is "*nán* 难", adjective，difficult, hard. You may say " *hěn nán* 很难", very difficult；"*bù nán* 不难", not hard.

难
［nán］
difficult/hard   adjective

For example：

- 汉语很难吗? ［Hànyǔ hěn nán ma］
  Is Chinese difficult?
- 汉语不难。［Hànyǔ bù nán］
  No，isn't.

Now let's learn something else.
We have learned that "*hǎo* 好 + Verb" to expresses that it's nice to do something.

好 + Verb
［hǎo］ + Verb

For example：

- 好吃 ［hǎo chī］
  delicious
- 好看 ［hǎo kàn］
  good-looking.
- 好听 ［hǎo tīng］
  nice to listen.

Today, let's change the "*hǎo* 好" to "*nán* 难", which changes the meaning "it's hard or difficult to do something."

For example：

- 难吃 [nán chī]

  hard to eat. (It tastes awful)

- 难看 [nán kàn]

  hard to look, ugly (ugly).

- 难听 [nán tīng]

  hard to listen, unpleasant to the ears.

OK, let's do some exercises.

to review what we have learned today.

- 今天的早饭很难吃。

  [Jīntiān de zǎofàn hěn nánchī]

  Today's breakfast is not delicious.

- 汉语很难，我的汉语不好。

  [Hànyǔ hěn nán, wǒ de Hànyǔ bù hǎo]

  Chinese is difficult, and my Chinese is poor.

- 你好，我姓李，我叫李娜。

  [Nǐ hǎo, wǒ xìng Lǐ, wǒ jiào Lǐ Nà]

  Hello, I'm Li Na.

- 朋友们都喜欢做饭。

  [Péngyǒu men dōu xǐhuan zuòfàn]

  They all like cooking.

Great, so that wraps up today's lesson. Hope you have learned something. Download our app to access our Chinese lessons. Remember you can learn Chinese anywhere, anytime with *ChineseAny*.

◯ **Word List**

Main Vocabulary		
姓[xìng] Surname; family name	朋友[péngyou] friend	难[nán] difficult
Additional Vocabulary		
好朋友[hǎo péngyou] good friend	难看[nán kàn] ugly	
难吃[nán chī] hard to eat (taste awful)	难听[nán tīng] hard to listen (unpleasant to listen)	

◯ **Notes**

难[nán] + verb：it's hard or difficult to do something.

E.g. ● 这个很难做。[Zhège hěn nán zuò]

It's hard to do this.

● 汉字很难学。[Hànzì hěn nán xué]

It's difficult to learn Chinese characters.

● 今天的早饭很难吃。[Jīntiān de zǎofàn hěn nánchī]

Today's breakfast is not delicious.

Quiz

I. Pronunciation.

1. Please choose the initials or finals you heard.

1) A. niǎo   B. liǎo

2) A. quán   B. qián

3) A. guò   B. duò

4) A. bēi   B. biē

2. Please choose the Pinyin you heard.

1) A. péngyou   B. píngguǒ

2) A. nánde   B. nándé

3) A. nánkàn   B. lángān

4) A. hǎochu   B. gāochù

II. Form sentences.

1. nǐ   míngzi   shénme   jiào
  1   2   3   4

_____

2. péngyou   tā   wǒ   de   shì   hǎo
   1   2   3   4   5   6

_____

3. hěn   dōngxi   nán   nàge   mǎi
  1   2   3   4   5

_____

4. nán   Hànyǔ   hěn   xué
  1   2   3   4

_____

III. Please translate the following sentences into Chinese.

1. What is your friend's name?

   _____

2. Her good friend can speak a little Chinese.

   _____

3. It is very difficult to buy that movie ticket.

   _____

4. What is your teacher's surname?

   _____

This One or That One

Welcome to Elementary Level Two, Lesson Four of our **ChineseAny** podcast series teaching Chinese. Today we will learn three vocabularies, one conjunction, one verb and one noun. Let's look at them now.

The 1st vocabulary, "*háishì* 还是", conjunction, "or". You may only use that in an alternative question, such as "A or B?".

还是
[háishì]
or   conjunction

For example：

- 你想喝什么,咖啡还是茶? [Nǐ xiǎng hē shénme, kāfēi háishì chá]
  What would you like to drink, coffee or tea?

- 你是中国人还是韩国人? [Nǐ shì Zhōngguó rén háishì Hánguó rén]
  Are you Chinese or Korean?

- 你今天学习还是明天学习? [Nǐ jīntiān xuéxí háishì míngtiān xuéxí]
  Will you study today or tomorrow?

OK, the 2nd character is, "*xiě* 写" "to write".

写
[xiě]
to write   verb

For example：
- 写汉字 [xiě Hànzì]
  write Chinese character

- 我说，你写。［Wǒ shuō, nǐ xiě］
  I speak, and you write.
- 我可以说汉语，不可以写汉字。［Wǒ kěyǐ shuō hànyǔ, bù kěyǐ xiě Hànzì］
  I can speak Chinese, but cannot write Chinese characters.

OK, today's 3rd word is "*shuǐguǒ 水果*", fruit.

> 水果
> ［shuǐguǒ］
> **fruit** noun

For example：
- 你喜欢吃水果吗？［Nǐ xǐhuān chī shuǐguǒ ma］
  Do you like to eat fruit?
- 你喜欢吃什么水果？［Nǐ xǐhuān chī shénme shuǐguǒ］
  What fruit do you like to eat?

For the fruit names，Please check the vocabulary form attached to find your favorite fruit.

> 西瓜
> ［xīguā］
> **watermelon** noun

> 猕猴桃
> ［mí hóu táo］
> **kiwi** noun

> 桃子
> ［táozi］
> **peach** noun

> 橙子
> ［chéngzi］
> **orange** noun

櫻桃
[yīngtáo]
cherry   noun

甜瓜
[tiánguā]
melon   noun

苹果
[píngguǒ]
apple   noun

葡萄
[pútáo]
grape   noun

酸橙
[suānchéng]
lime   noun

Let's try to translate the following sentences into Chinese to review today's lesson.

● 你喜欢上海还是北京?
[Nǐ xǐhuān Shànghǎi háishì Běijīng]
Do you like Shanghai or Beijing?

● 你要这个还是那个?
[Nǐ yào zhège háishì nàge]
You want this one or that one?

● 说汉语不难,写汉字很难。
[Shuō hànyǔ bù nán,xiě hànzì hěn nán]
Speaking Chinese is easy, but writing it is hard.

● 今天买还是明天买?
[Jīntiān mǎi háishì míngtiān mǎi]
You want to buy it today or tomorrow?

Great, so that wraps up today's lesson. Hope you have learned something. Download our app to access our Chinese lessons, Remember you can learn Chinese anywhere, anytime with **ChineseAny**.

Word List

Main Vocabulary		
还是[háishi] or	写[xiě] to write	水果[shuǐguǒ] fruit
Additional Vocabulary		
西瓜[xīguā] watermelon	猕猴桃[míhóu táo] kiwi	桃子[táozi] peach
橙子[chéngzi] orange	樱桃[yīngtáo] cherry	甜瓜[tiánguā] melon
苹果[píngguǒ] apple	葡萄[pútáo] grape	酸橙[suānchéng] lime

Notes

"还是[háishì]", conjunction "or":

You may only use that in an alternative question, such as A or B?

e. g. ● 你想吃什么,面包还是米饭? [Nǐ xiǎng hē shénme, miànbāo háishi mǐfàn]

What would you like to eat, bread or rice?

　　● 你是学生还是老师? [Nǐshì xuéshēng háishi lǎoshī]

Are you a student or a teacher?

Quiz

I. Pronunciation.

1. Please choose the initials or finals you heard.

   1) A. xiě   B. xuě

   2) A. kū   B. gū

   3) A. bāng   B. bān

   4) A. fà   B. fàn

2. Please choose the Pinyin you heard.

   1) A. háishì   B. kāishǐ

   2) A. shuǐguǒ   B. zhùguo

   3) A. xiězì   B. xuēzi

   4) A. niánjì   B. niánjí

II. Form sentences.

1. chá   yào   háishi   nǐ   kāfēi
   1   2   3   4   5

   _____

2. kěyǐ   nǐ   Hànzì   ma   xiě
   1   2   3   4   5

   _____

3. shuǐguǒ   hěn   zhège   hǎochī
   1   2   3   4

   _____

4. xǐhuān   shuǐguǒ   nǐ   shénme
   1   2   3   4

   _____

III. Please translate the following sentences into Chinese.

1. What do you call this fruit?

_____

2. Do you like to speak Chinese or write Chinese character?

_____

3. Does she like to drink coffee or tea?

_____

4. Writing Chinese character is very difficult.

_____

Please

Welcome to Elementary Level Two, Lesson Five of our **ChineseAny** podcast series teaching Chinese. This is Lesson 5. In today's lesson, we will learn three useful verbs.

The 1st one, "*qǐng* 请".

"*qǐng* 请" has two meanings in Chinese.

> 请
> [qǐng]
> please   verb

The 1st meaning is "please".

We normally use it before a **VERB**, to express "please do something" in a polite way.

> 请 + Verb
> [qǐng]
> please

For example：

- 请喝水。[Qǐng hē shuǐ]
  Please have water.
- 请说英语。[Qǐng shuō yīngyǔ]
  Please speak English.

The 2nd meaning for "*qǐng* 请" is to invite somebody to do something.

For example：

- 他想请我吃晚饭。［Tā xiǎng qǐng wǒ chī wǎnfàn］
  He would like to invite me for dinner.
- 我（想）请你喝咖啡。［Wǒ（xiǎng）qǐng nǐ hē kāfēi］
  I want to invite you for coffee.

OK, the 2nd verb is "*wèn* 问", "to ask a question".

So, when you ask a question, such as "May I ask?" or "Excuse me", in Chinese you should begin with "*qǐng wèn* 请问" which is followed by your question.

For example：

- 请问，你可以说汉语吗？［Qǐng wèn, nǐ kěyǐ shuō hànyǔ ma］
  Excuse me, can you speak Chinese?
- 请问，这是茶吗？［Qǐng wèn, zhè shì chá ma］
  Excuse me, is this tea?

| 问 |
| [wèn] |
| to ask   verb |

Let's move on to our 3rd word "*qù* 去", to go.

| 去 |
| [qù] |
| to go   verb |

When we use it, we must have a **LOCATION** after it.

| 去 + Location |
| [qù] |
| to go |

For example,
- 去北京［qù Běijīng］
  go to Beijing

● 去德国［qù Déguó］
go to Germany

Let's try to translate the following sentences into Chinese to review today's lesson.

> ● 我的好朋友想去中国学汉语。
> ［Wǒ de hǎo péngyǒu xiǎng qù Zhōngguó xué hànyǔ］
> My good friend would like to go to China to learn Chinese.

> ● 请问，你想去上海吗?
> ［Qǐng wèn, nǐ xiǎng qù Shànghǎi ma?］
> Excuse me, do you want to go to Shanghai?

> ● 他问你什么?
> ［Tā wèn nǐ shénme?］
> What did he ask you?

> ● 我请朋友们看电影。
> ［Wǒ qǐng péngyǒu men kàn diànyǐng］
> I invite my friends to watch a movie.

> ● 请问，这个是什么?
> ［Qǐng wèn, zhège shì shénme?］
> Excuse me, what is this?

Great, so that wraps up today's lesson. Hope you have learned something. Download our app to access our Chinese lessons. Remember, you can learn Chinese anywhere, anytime with **ChineseAny**.

Word List

Main Vocabulary		
请[qǐng] please；to ask；to invite	问[wèn] to ask	去[qù] to go

Notes

请[qǐng]：**please；to invite**

➤ **请**[qǐng] **+ verb：to do something in a polite way.**

e.g. ● 请不要客气。[Qǐng búyào kèqi]

Please don't be polite.

● 请喝茶。[Qǐng hē chá]

Please have some tea.

➤ **请**[qǐng] **+ somebody + verb：to invite somebody to do something.**

e.g. ● 他想请我看电影。[Tā xiǎng qǐng wǒ kàn diànyǐng]

He would like to invite me for a movie.

● 我想请你喝德国啤酒。[Wǒ xiǎng qǐng nǐ hē Déguó píjiǔ]

I want to invite you to have German beer.

Quiz

I. Pronunciation.

1. Please choose the initials or finals you heard.

1) A. guān   B. kuān

2) A. gēn   B. gēng

3) A. luò   B. lòu

4) A. yē   B. niē

2. Please choose the Pinyin you heard.

1) A. qíngkuàng   B. jìnkuàng

2) A. wēndù   B. wěidù

3) A. qùwèi   B. jùhuì

4) A. chāoshì   B. zhāoshì

II. Form sentences.

1. lǎoshī nǐ shénme wèn
  1 2 3   4

_____

2. qǐng nǐ wèn xǐhuan shénme chī
  1 2 3 4   5   6

_____

3. qǐng jīntiān wǒ chī tā wǔfàn
  1   2 3 4 5 6

_____

4. qù nǐ xiǎng ma Běijīng
  1 2 3 4 5

_____

III. Please translate the following sentences into Chinese.

1. What do you like to do?

_____

2. What do you want to study?

_____

3. Do you go to Beijing or Shanghai?

_____

4. Please speak Chinese.

_____

I'm at Home

Welcome to Elementary Level Two, Lesson Six of our **ChineseAny** podcast series teaching Mandarin Chinese. Today we will learn three new vocabularies: one conjunction, one verb and one noun. Let's look at them now.

The 1st one, "*zài* 在", to be at, in, on ... and so on.

> 在
> [zài]
> to be at, in ...
> Conjunction

We usually use it before a **PLACE** to express the location.

> 在 + Place
> [zài]
> to be at, in ...

For example:
- 在中国 [zài Zhōngguó]
  In China
- 在上海 [zài Shànghǎi]
  In Shanghai

"*zài* 在" has some other meanings. We will learn them in the future.

OK, let's learn two location-related words,
The 1st one is "*jiā* 家", home or family.

- 在家 [zài jiā]
  at home
- 在你的家 [zài nǐ de jiā]
  at your home
- 不在家 [bú zài jiā]
  not at home
- 家人 [jiā rén]
  home person, means family members.

家
[jiā]
home/family   noun

Let's see some sentences：

- 他们是我的家人。[Tāmen shì wǒ de jiārén]
  They are my family members.
- 我的家人都在上海。[Wǒ de jiārén dōu zài shànghǎi]
  My family members are all in Shanghai.

The 2nd location-related word is
"*shāngdiàn* 商店", shop or store.

"*shāng* 商" means "business", So could
you guess how to say businessman in Chinese?
That is "*shāngrén* 商人"

商店
[shāngdiàn]
shop, store   noun

"*diàn* 店" means "store, shop". The difference between "*shāng
diàn* 商店" and "*diàn* 店" is that "*shāngdiàn* 商店" can refer to any
store. "*diàn* 店" can describe a specific type of store if there is an
adjective before it.

For example：

- 咖啡店 [kāfēi diàn]
  coffee shop

- 面包店 [miànbāo diàn]

  bakery

- 饭店 [fàn diàn]

  restaurant

Let's try to translate the following sentences into Chinese to review today's lesson.

- 你今天在家吗?

  [Nǐ jīntiān zài jiā ma]

  Are you at home today?

- 明天我不在上海。

  [Míngtiān wǒ bú zài Shànghǎi]

  Tomorrow I'm not in Shanghai.

- 这个饭店的饭好吃。

  [Zhège fàndiàn de fàn hěn hǎochī]

  The food in this restaurant is delicious.

- 我请你在我家喝中国茶。

  [Wǒ qǐng nǐ zài wǒ jiā hē zhōngguó chá]

  I invite you to my home for Chinese tea.

- 请问,索菲在吗?

  [Qǐng wèn, Suǒfēi zài ma]

  Excuse me, is Sophie here?

- 早上我不在家吃早饭。

  [Zǎoshàng wǒ bú zài jiā chī zǎofàn]

  I don't have breakfast at home.

Great, so that wraps up today's lesson. Hope you have learned something. Download our app to access our Chinese lessons. Remember, you can learn Chinese anywhere, anytime with **ChineseAny**.

Word List

Main Vocabulary		
在[zài] to be at, in	家[jiā] home	商店[shāngdiàn] shop
Additional Vocabulary		
面包店[miànbāo diàn] bakery	饭店[fàndiàn] restaurant	咖啡店[kāfēi diàn] coffee shop
商人[shāngrén] businessman	家人[jiārén] family	

Notes

在[zài]：**be at；be in**

➤ **Statement sentence：subject + 在[zài] + place + verb**

e.g. ● 我在中国学习汉语。[Wǒ zài Zhōngguó xuéxí Hànyǔ]

I study Chinese in China.

● 我的家人都在上海。[Wǒ de jiārén dōu zài Shànghǎi]

My family members are all in Shanghai.

➤ **Negative sentence：subject + 不[bú] + 在[zài] + place + verb**

e.g. ● 我不在家吃早饭。[Wǒ bú zài jiā chī zǎofàn]

I don't have breakfast at home.

● 明天我不在上海。[Míngtiān wǒ bú zài Shànghǎi]
  Tomorrow I'm not in Shanghai.

➢ **Question sentence：subject ＋ 在**[zài] **＋ place ＋ 吗**[ma]**?**

e. g. ● 你明天在家吗?［Nǐ míngtiān zài jiā ma］
  Are you at home tomorrow?

  ● 请问，我的奶奶在吗? ［Qǐng wèn，wǒde nǎinai zài ma］
  Excuse me, is my grandma here?

Quiz

I. Pronunciation.

　　1. Please choose the initials or finals you heard.

　　　　1) A. lǎn 　　　　　　　　B. luǎn

　　　　2) A. yùn 　　　　　　　　B. lùn

　　　　3) A. gōng 　　　　　　　B. kōng

　　　　4) A. lèi 　　　　　　　　B. liè

　　2. Please choose the Pinyin you heard.

　　　　1) A. fàndiàn 　　　　　　B. fāngbiàn

　　　　2) A. jiātíng 　　　　　　B. jiādīng

　　　　3) A. kāfēi 　　　　　　　B. kāihuì

　　　　4) A. yídìng 　　　　　　B. yùdìng

II. Form sentences.

　　1. <u>míngtiān</u>　　<u>zài</u>　　<u>wànshang</u>　　<u>jiā</u>　　<u>ma</u>　　<u>nǐmen</u>
　　　　　1　　　　　2　　　　3　　　　4　　　5　　　　6

　　2. <u>dōngxi</u>　　<u>tā</u>　　<u>qù</u>　　<u>shāngdiàn</u>　　<u>mǎi</u>
　　　　　1　　　　2　　　3　　　　4　　　　5

3. lǎoshī   lǎojiā   **Sophie**   zài   de   Hā'ěrbīn
  1   2   3   4   5   6

_____

4. wǒ   qù   kāfēi diàn   bú   nàge
  1   2   3   4   5

_____

III. Please translate the following sentences into Chinese.

1. Is Sophie here?

_____

2. I invite them to eat dinner at home.

_____

3. She does not like to cook at home.

_____

4. Do you want to eat at home or in the restaurant?

_____

I Come from China

Welcome to Elementary Level Two, Lesson Seven of our **ChineseAny** podcast series teaching Chinese. Today we will learn three new vocabularies: one pronoun and two verbs. Let's look at them now.

The 1st vocabulary, "*nǎlǐ 哪里*", "where". It's a special question word. The people from northern China also say "*nǎr 哪儿*"

- 在哪里[zài nǎlǐ], 在哪儿[zài nǎr]
  Be where
- 你在哪里? [Nǐ zài nǎlǐ] or 你在哪儿? [Nǐ zài nǎr]
  Where are you?
- 你的家在哪里? [Nǐ de jiā zài nǎlǐ]
  Where is your home?

Please remember the following sentence patterns when you use "where".

① **Sb./place** + *zài nǎlǐ 在哪里*?
means "Where is somebody or someting"?

$$\text{sb./place} + \begin{cases} \text{在哪里} \\ [\text{zài nǎlǐ}] \\ \text{在哪儿} \\ [\text{zài nàr}] \end{cases}$$

② **Sb.** + *zài nǎlǐ* 在哪里 **+ to do something.** means "Sb. is doing something at some place."

> sb. + 在哪里 + to do sth.
>
> [zài nǎlǐ]

③ **Sb.** + *qù nǎlǐ* 去哪里 **+ to do something.** means "Sb. is going to some place to do something."

> sb. + 去哪里 + to do sth.
>
> [qù nǎlǐ]

The 2nd word is "*zhù* 住", to live.

Live in, at, on **+ PLACE** in Chinese should be "*zhù zài* 住在 + *Place* "

> 住
>
> [zhù]
>
> to live   verb

For example：
- 我住在上海。[Wǒ zhù zài Shànghǎi]
  I live in Shanghai.
- 你住在哪儿? [Nǐ zhù zài nǎr]
  Where do you live?

The last word for today is "*zuò* 坐", to sit.

> 坐
>
> [zuò]
>
> to sit   verb

- 请坐 [Qǐng zuò]
  Please sit down
- 你坐在哪儿? [Nǐ zuò zài nǎr]
  Where do you sit?

Great, let's try to translate the following sentences into Chinese to review today's lesson.

● 请问,在哪儿写名字?
[Qǐng wèn, zài nǎr xiě míngzì]
Excuse me, where do I write my name?

● 我喜欢住在上海。
[Wǒ xǐhuān zhù zài Shànghǎi]
I like living in Shanghai.

● 你去哪里学习汉语?
[Nǐ qù nǎlǐ xuéxí hànyǔ]
Where do you learn Chinese?

● 他今天晚上在哪里吃晚饭?
[Tā jīntiān wǎnshàng zài nǎlǐ chī wǎnfàn]
Where will he have dinner tonight?

Great, so that wraps up today's lesson. Hope you learned something. Download our app to access our Chinese lessons. Remember, you can learn Chinese anywhere, anytime with **ChineseAny**.

Word List

Main Vocabulary		
哪里[nǎlǐ] where	住[zhù] to live; to stay	坐[zuò] to sit
Additional Vocabulary		
哪儿[nǎr] where		

◔ Notes

Question mark：哪里[nǎlǐ]**where**

➤ **Sb.\Place + 在**[zài]**哪里**[nǎlǐ]**\在**[zài]**哪儿**[nǎr]

e. g. ● 你在哪里? [Nǐ zài nǎlǐ]

Where are you?

● 你的家在哪里? [Nǐ de jiā zài nǎlǐ]

Where is your home?

➤ **Sb. + 在**[zài]**+ 哪里**[nǎlǐ]**+ verb + object**

e. g. ● 你在哪里学习汉语? [Nǐ zài nǎlǐ xuéxí Hànyǔ]

Where do you study Chinese?

● 他今天晚上在哪里吃晚饭? [Tā jīntiān wǎnshang zài nǎlǐ chī wǎnfàn]

Where will he have dinner tonight?

➤ **Sb. + 去**[qù]**+ 哪里**[nǎlǐ]**+ verb + object**

e. g. ● 你去哪里吃中国饭? [Nǐ qù nǎlǐ chī Zhōngguó fàn]

Where do you eat Chinese food?

● 你去哪里喝咖啡? [Nǐ qù nǎlǐ hē kāfēi]

Where do you drink coffee?

◔ Quiz

I. Pronunciation.

1. Please choose the initials or finals you heard.

1) A. pǐ   B. bǐ

2) A. nián   B. lián

3) A. huī   B. kuī

4) A. xióng   B. qióng

2. Please choose the Pinyin you heard.

1) A. zhùhù   B. zūhù

2) A. lìzi   B. lízi

3) A. zhuōzi   B. zhuózi

4) A. kānhù   B. gànbù

II. Form sentences.

1. nǐ   zài   xǐhuan   chī   nǎlǐ   wǎnfàn
   1   2   3   4   5   6

_____

2. zài   qǐng   nǐ   zhù   nǎlǐ   wèn
   1   2   3   4   5   6

_____

3. nǐ   zài   xiǎng   nǎlǐ   mǎi
   1   2   3   4   5

_____

4. zài   wǒ   Shànghǎi   Hànyǔ   xuéxí
   1   2   3   4   5

_____

III. Please translate the following sentences into Chinese.

1. Where do you study Chinese?

_____

2. Please sit down, please drink tea.

_____

3. I like to live in Shanghai, and you?

_____

4. Where can I buy Chinese tea?

_____

I'm Here

Welcome to Elementary Level Two, Lesson Eight of our **ChineseAny** podcast series teaching Chinese. Today we will learn three nouns.

The 1st vocabulary is "*xǐshǒu jiān* 洗手间", "washroom or bathroom".

"*xǐ* 洗" means "to wash", "*shǒu* 手" means "hand", "*jiān* 间" means "room", the room to wash hands.

> 洗手间
> [xǐshǒu jiān]
> washroom/bathroom   noun

You're getting two additional new words from this：

"*xǐ* 洗", "to wash", you may say "*xǐ shuǐguǒ* 洗水果", "to wash the fruit".

"*shǒu* 手", "hand", you may say "*wǒ de shǒu* 我的手", "my hands".

OK, let's go back to the word "washroom/bathroom".
"Where is the washroom/bathroom, please?"
"*Qǐng wèn, xǐshǒu jiān zài nǎr* 请问,洗手间在哪儿？"
That's a commonly-used sentence. Please remember it.

OK, let's move on to the 2nd character, "*lái* 来", "to come".

> 来
> [lái]
> To come   verb

Normally, we put a **LOCATION** after it to express "come somewhere to do something".

来 + Place + to do sth.
[lái]

For example,
- 来上海[lái Shànghǎi]
  come to Shanghai.
- 来我的家[lái wǒ de jiā]
  come to my home.

The 3rd word of today's lesson is a preposition "*cóng* 从", "from".

从
[cóng]
from   preposition

Normally we use it with "*lái* 来" to express "come back from some place".

从 + place + 来
[cóng]   [lái]
from   come

For example,
- 我从中国来。[Wǒ cóng Zhōngguó lái]
  I come from China.
- 你从哪儿来? [Nǐ cóng nǎr lái]
  Where are you from?

Great, let's try to translate the following sentences into Chinese to review today's lesson.

● 我的朋友想来上海看我。

[Wǒde péngyǒu xiǎng lái Shànghǎi kàn wǒ]

My friend would like to come to Shanghai to see me.

● 你的汉语老师从哪儿来？

[Nǐ de hànyǔ lǎoshī cóng nǎr lái]

Where does your Chinese teacher come from?

● 她从哈尔滨来上海。

[Tā cóng Hāěrbīn lái Shànghǎi]

She comes to Shanghai from Harbin.

● 明天我的家人从丹麦来上海。

[Míngtiān wǒ de jiārén cóng Dānmài lái Shànghǎi]

My families will come to Shanghai from Denmark tomorrow.

● 你要洗什么？

[Nǐ yào xǐ shénme]

What do you want to wash?

● 你的手很好看。

[Nǐ de shǒu hěn hǎokàn]

Your hands are beautiful.

Great, so that wraps up today's lesson. Hope you have learned something. Download our app to access our Chinese lessons. Remember, you can learn Chinese anywhere, anytime with **ChineseAny**.

Word List

Main Vocabulary		
洗手间［xǐshǒujiān］ toilet；W. C	来［lái］ to come	从［cóng］ from
Additional Vocabulary		
洗［xǐ］ to wash	手［shǒu］ hand	间［jiān］ room

Notes

The preposition，"从［cóng］"

从［cóng］ **+ place + 来**［lái］

e. g. ● 你从中国来吗?［Nǐ cóng Zhōngguó lái ma］

   Are you from China?

   ● 你从哪儿来?［Nǐ cóng nǎr lái］

   Where are you from?

Quiz

I. Pronunciation.

   1. Please choose the initials or finals you heard.

   1）A. méng   B. néng

   2）A. jiān   B. jiāng

3) A. shuō   B. shōu

4) A. yē   B. jiē

2. Please choose the Pinyin you heard.

1) A. zhùyì   B. zhǔyì

2) A. měijiàn   B. měitiān

3) A. zàijiàn   B. zhàiquàn

4) A. guānxì   B. guānxīn

II. Form sentences.

1. <u>lái</u>   <u>wǒ de</u>   <u>lǎoshī</u>   <u>cóng</u>   <u>Hànyǔ</u>   <u>Hā'ěrbīn</u>
    1   2   3   4   5   6

2. <u>Běijīng</u>   <u>kàn</u>   <u>tāmne</u>   <u>cóng</u>   <u>lái</u>   <u>Shànghǎi</u>   <u>wǒ</u>
    1   2   3   4   5   6   7

3. <u>jiārén</u>   <u>Zhōngguó</u>   <u>lái</u>   <u>wǒ de</u>   <u>míngtiān</u>
    1   2   3   4   5

4. <u>tā</u>   <u>qù</u>   <u>xǐshǒujiān</u>   <u>xiǎng</u>
    1   2   3   4

III. Please translate the following sentences into Chinese.

1. Where do you come from?

2. Excuse me, where is the toilet?

3. I come from my home.

4. My friend wants to come to China to learn Chinese.

My Job

Welcome to Elementary Level Two, Lesson Nine of our **ChineseAny** podcast series teaching Mandarin Chinese. Today we will learn three nouns. Let's start.

The 1st vocabulary, "*gōngzuò* 工作" job, work. "*gōngzuò* 工作" can be both a noun and a verb.

> 工作
> [gōngzuò]
> Work, job   Noun/verb

As a noun, you may say "*zuò gōngzuò* 做工作", do a job, do work.

As a verb, you may say, "*zài nǎr gōngzuò？* 在哪儿工作?", where do you work?

For example,

- 你做什么工作? [Nǐ zuò shénme gōngzuò]
  What job do you do?
- 这个工作很难。[Zhège gōngzuò hěn nán]
  This job is difficult.
- 你喜欢这个工作吗? [Nǐ xǐhuān zhège gōngzuò ma]
  Do you like this job?

OK, let's see the next two words, "here and there".

"*zhèlǐ* 这里", here；"*nàlǐ* 那里", there. Normally, we also say "*zhèr* 这儿" and "*nàr* 那儿" verbally.

Please pay attention to the difference in tone between "*nàlǐ 那里*" there, and "*nǎlǐ 哪里*" where.

Normally we add the preposition "*zài 在*" before them to express "to be here" or "to be there".

"*zài zhèr 在这儿*", "be here"

"*zài nàr 在那儿*", "be there".

For example：

- 请坐在这儿［Qǐng zuò zài zhèr］

  Please sit here

- 他在那儿吃早饭。［Tā zài nàr chī zǎofàn］

  He is there eating breakfast. (He is eating breakfast there)

When we express "there is" or "isn't something here or there", you may use "*zhèlǐ 这里/nàlǐ 那里 + yǒu 有+ something*", or "*zhèlǐ 这里/nàlǐ 那里+ méiyǒu 没有+something*".

> 这里/那里 + 有 + sth.
> [zhèlǐ] [nàlǐ] [yǒu]
> 这里/那里 + 没有 + sth.
> [zhèlǐ] [nàlǐ] [méiyǒu]

For example：

- 这里没有咖啡店。［Zhèlǐ méiyǒu kāfēi diàn］

  There is no coffee shop here.

- 那里有洗手间。［Nàlǐ yǒu xǐshǒu jiān］

  There is a washroom/bathroom there.

So, please remember, when we use "**there be**" sentences, the "*zài 在*" before "*zhèlǐ 这里/nàlǐ 那里*" could be omitted. In the example above, "there is no coffee shop here" you don't need to say "*zài zhèlǐ méiyǒu kāfēi diàn 在这里没有咖啡店*", you just need to say "*zhèlǐ méiyǒu kāfēi diàn 这里没有咖啡店*".

Great, let's try to translate the following sentences into Chinese to review today's lesson.

● 那里没有商店。

[Nàlǐ méiyǒu shāngdiàn]

There is no shop there.

● 我们可以坐在这里吗?

[Wǒmen kěyǐ zuò zài zhèlǐ ma]

Can we sit here?

● 明天我们去那儿工作。

[Míngtiān wǒmen qù nàr gōngzuò]

We shall go there for work tomorrow.

● 请问,哪里有洗手间?

[Qǐng wèn, nǎlǐ yǒu xǐshǒu jiān]

Excuse me, where is the washroom?

Great, so that wraps up today's lesson. Hope you have learned something. Download our app to access our Chinese lessons. Remember, you can learn Chinese anywhere, anytime with **ChineseAny**.

◖ **Word List**

Main Vocabulary		
工作[gōngzuò] to work; job	这里[zhèlǐ] here	那里[nàlǐ] there
Additional Vocabulary		
这儿[zhèr] here	那儿[nàr] there	

◖ Notes

Sentences indicating existence

这里[zhèlǐ]
那里[nàlǐ]　+ ⎫有[yǒu]/没有[méiyǒu] + **noun**
哪里[nǎlǐ]　　⎭

e. g. ● 这里有咖啡店。[Zhèlǐ yǒu kāfēi diàn]

Here is a coffee shop.

　　● 请问,哪里有商店? [Qǐng wèn, nǎlǐ yǒu shāngdiàn]

Excuse me, where is the shop?

　　● 那里没有商店。[Nàlǐ méiyǒu shāngdiàn]

There is no shop there.

◖ Quiz

I. Pronunciation.

　1. Please choose the initials or finals you heard.

　　1) A. zè　　　　　　　　B. zhè

　　2) A. zuǒ　　　　　　　B. zǒu

　　3) A. qī　　　　　　　　B. chī

　　4) A. sàng　　　　　　　B. shàng

　2. Please choose the Pinyin you heard.

　　1) A. nǎlǐ　　　　　　　B. nàlǐ

　　2) A. gòngxiàn　　　　　B. gòngxiǎng

　　3) A. shànghǎi　　　　　B. shānghài

　　4) A. zuòzhe　　　　　　B. zǒuzhe

148

II. Form sentences.

1. nǐ   ma   gōngzuò   māma
   1   2   3   4

_____

2. zhèlǐ   tā   zuò   xiǎng   zài
   1   2   3   4   5

_____

3. wǒ de   zài   jiā   nàlǐ
   1   2   3   4

_____

4. wǒ   zhège   xǐhuan   hěn   gōngzuò
   1   2   3   4   5

_____

III. Please translate the following sentences into Chinese.

1. What kind of job do you do?

_____

2. Where do you work?

_____

3. Can I sit here?

_____

4. Do you like to work here or there?

_____

Where Is the Airport

You are learning Mandarin Chinese with **ChineseAny.** This is Elementary Level Two, Lesson Ten of our podcast series. Today we will learn three new vocabulary words: two nouns and one verb. Let's look at them now.

The 1st one, "*jīchǎng 机场*", airport. "*jī 机*" means "machine or airplane".

"*chǎng 场*" means "square, airplane square", "*jīchǎng 机场*" means "airport".

"in airport", "*zài jīchǎng 在机场*"; "go to airport", "*qù jīchǎng 去机场*".

机场
[jīchǎng]
airport   noun

The 2nd word is "*chē 车*", car.

- 你的车 [nǐ de chē]
  your car
- 我的车 [wǒ de chē]
  my car
- 我有车。[nǐ yǒu chē]
  You have a car.
- 我没有车。[wǒ méiyǒu chē]
  I don't have car.

For example:

车
[chē]
car   noun

- 他买车。[Tā mǎi chē]

  He buys a car.

- 你的车很好看。[Nǐ de chē hěn hǎokàn]

  Your car is nice.

Great, let's look at the 3rd character, "*tíng* 停", to stop.

停
[tíng]
to stop   verb

"*tíng chē* 停车" means "to stop the car or to park".

Just now, we learned that "*chǎng* 场" means "square". So can you guess how to say "parking lot"?

Yes, that is "*tíngchē chǎng* 停车场".

Let's see some examples:

- 我在停车场。[Wǒ zài tíngchē chǎng]

  I'm in the parking lot.

- 请在这儿停车。[Qǐng zài zhèr tíngchē]

  Stop the car here, please.

Great, now let's learn something that will be used in conventional conversation.

- We previously learned that "*shǒu* 手" means "hands", and today we learned "*jī* 机" means "machine". So what's the meaning of "hand machine"? Yes, that's hand phone, mobile phone, "*shǒu jī* 手机"

- Previously we learned "*shuǐ* 水", which means "water", and today we learned "*tíng* 停", "to stop". So can you guess the meaning of "*tíng shuǐ* 停水" in Chinese? Yes, that is "shut off the water".

Let's try to translate the following sentences into Chinese to review today's lesson.

● 请问，机场在哪里？
  [Qǐng wèn, jīchǎng zài nǎlǐ]
  Excuse me, where is the airport?

● 这里可以停车吗？
  [Zhèlǐ kěyǐ tíngchē ma]
  Can I park here?

● 明天我去洗车。
  [Míngtiān wǒ qù xǐ chē]
  Tomorrow I will go to wash the car.

● 这个车是你的吗？
  [Zhège chē shì nǐ de ma]
  Is this car yours?

● 你去浦东机场还是虹桥机场？
  [Nǐ qù Pǔdōng jīchǎng háishì Hóngqiáo jīchǎng]
  Will you go to Pudong airport or Hongqiao airport?

Great, so that wraps up today's lesson. Hope you have learned something. Download our app to learn Chinese anywhere, anytime with **ChineseAny**.

Word List

Main Vocabulary		
机场[jīchǎng] airport	车[chē] car	停[tíng] to stop
Additional Vocabulary		
手机[shǒujī] mobile phone	停水[tíng shuǐ] shut off the water	停车场[tíngchēchǎng] parking lot

Notes

Chinese sentence's order：

Time ＋ subject ＋ Place ＋ way ＋ verb ＋ object

Subject ＋ Time ＋ Place ＋ way ＋ verb ＋ object

e. g. ● 我明天在机场见朋友。［Wǒ míngtiān zài jīchǎng jiàn péngyou］

I will meet my friend at the airport.

● 明天我去洗车。［Míngtiān wǒ qù xǐ chē］

Tomorrow I will go to wash the car.

● 朋友们喜欢在饭店吃饭。［Péngyou men xǐhuan zài fàndiàn chīfàn］

My friends like to eat food in the restaurant.

Quiz

Ⅰ. Pronunciation.

1. Please choose the initials or finals you heard.

　　1）A. jī　　　　　　　　　B. qī

　　2）A. tíng　　　　　　　　B. qíng

　　3）A. lái　　　　　　　　　B. léi

　　4）A. nù　　　　　　　　　B. lù

2. Please choose the Pinyin you heard.

　　1）A. jīchǎng　　　　　　　B. qìchǎng

　　2）A. shōují　　　　　　　　B. shǒuqì

　　3）A. qìchē　　　　　　　　B. xǐchē

　　4）A. miànqián　　　　　　　B. miànjiàn

II. Form sentences.

1. <u>qǐng</u> <u>nǎlǐ</u> <u>wèn</u> <u>zài</u> <u>chē</u> <u>wǒmen</u> <u>xià</u>
    1   2   3   4   5   6   7

2. <u>wǒ</u> <u>jiàn</u> <u>jīchǎng</u> <u>qù</u> <u>péngyou</u>
    1   2   3   4   5

3. <u>tíng</u> <u>zhèlǐ</u> <u>nǐ</u> <u>bù</u> <u>chē</u> <u>kěyǐ</u> <u>zài</u>
    1   2   3   4   5   6   7

4. <u>lǐ</u> <u>wǒ de</u> <u>zài</u> <u>shǒujī</u> <u>chē</u>
    1   2   3   4   5

III. Please translate the following sentences into Chinese.

1. Where do I get off?

2. Can I park the car here?

3. Your car is very nice.

4. She works at Pudong airport.

Taxi

Welcome to Elementary Level Two, Lesson Eleven of **ChineseAny** podcast series teaching Mandarin Chinese. Today we will learn three new vocabulary words: two verbs and one noun.

The 1st word is "*zhīdào* 知道", "to know". "*zhīdào* 知道" is a **VERB**.

知道
[zhīdào]
to know   verb

You may put what you know after. "知道" which can be a **NOUN** or **clause**.

The negative form of "*zhīdào* 知道" is "**bù zhīdào** 不知道", it means "don't know".

知道
[zhīdào] + { noun
sentence
clause }

For example:
- 我知道你的名字。[Wǒ zhīdào nǐ de míngzì]
  I know your name?
- 我不知道你是美国人。[Wǒ bù zhīdào nǐ shì Měiguó rén]
  I don't know you are from USA.
- 你知道吗? [Nǐ zhīdào ma]
  Do you know?

The 2nd word is "*zuò* 坐", In Lesson Seven, we have learned "*zuò* 坐" already which means "to sit". But today we will learn the 2nd meaning it has when it is used as a **preposition** followed by a mode of transport.

> 坐
> [zuò]
> to sit   verb

We use "*zuò* 坐 + *the mode of transport*" to express that you've gone or come to some place by taxi, bus, subway, airplane and so on.

> 坐 + the mode of
> [zuò]
> transport

Previously, we learned that the basic Chinese sentence structure is：

Subject + Time word + Place word + Verb + Object

But, when you need to include the transportation method in the sentence to describe the verb or action, you have to put it before the verb.

Subject + Time word + Place word + the transportation method + Verb + Object

Let's look at an example：

● 他今天从美国来中国。[Tā jīntiān cóng Měiguó lái Zhōngguó]

He is coming to China from America today.

If we choose a transportation means, take an airplane "*zuò fēijī* 坐飞机", we **MUST** put it before the **VERB**, to come from, "*cóng ... lái* 从……来".

● 他今天坐飞机从美国来中国。[Tā jīntiān zuò fēijī cóng Měiguó lái Zhōngguó]

He takes an airplane from America to China today.

The 3rd word is taxi, "*chūzū chē 出租车*". "*chū 出*" is (get) out; "*zū 租*" is to rent, "*chūzū 出租*" (out) rent; "*chē 车*" means "car, rent car"; "*chūzū chē 出租车*", taxi; Take taxi, "*zuò chūzū chē 坐出租车*".

出租车
[chūzū chē]
taxi   noun

For example：

- 坐出租车去机场 [Zuò chūzū chē qù jīchǎng]
  Go to airport by taxi.

- 坐出租车来我家 [Zuò chūzū chē lái wǒ jiā]
  Take a taxi/cab to my house.

Great, let's try to translate the following sentences into Chinese to review today's lesson.

- 我知道他不喜欢喝咖啡。
  [Wǒ zhīdào tā bù xǐhuan hē kāfēi]
  I know he doesn't like to drink coffee.

- 你知道这个吗?
  [Nǐ zhīdào zhège ma]
  Do you know this?

- 对不起,你的车不可以停在这里。
  [Duìbuqǐ, nǐ de chē bù kěyǐ tíng zài zhèlǐ]
  Sorry, you can't park your car here.

● 早上我坐出租车去工作。

[Zǎoshang wǒ zuò chūzū chē qù gōngzuò]

In the morning, I take the taxi/cab to work.

● 你知道在哪里停车吗?

[Nǐ zhīdào zài nǎlǐ tíngchē ma]

Do you know where to park?

● 你喜欢坐什么车?

[Nǐ xǐhuan zuò shénme chē]

What car do you like to ride in?

● 我不知道他叫什么。

[Wǒ bù zhīdào tā jiào shénme]

I don't know his name.

Great, so that wraps up today's lesson. Hope you have learned something useful today. You can download our app to access all of our Chinese lessons and learn Chinese anywhere, anytime with **ChineseAny**.

Word List

Main Vocabulary		
知道[zhīdào] to know	坐[zuò] to take	出租车[chūzū chē] taxi
Additional Vocabulary		
出[chū] out	租[zū] to rent	出租[chūzū] to (out) rent

Notes

① 知道[zhīdào]

➢ **Statement sentence：subject + 知道[zhīdào] + object**

e.g. ● 我知道他是你的汉语老师。[Wǒ zhīdào tā shì nǐ de Hànyǔ lǎoshī]

I know he is your Chinese teacher.

● 我们知道他不喜欢喝茶。[Wǒmen zhīdào tā bù xǐhuan hē chá]

We know he does not like to drink tea.

➢ **Negative sentence：subject + 不[bù] + 知道[zhīdào] + object**

e.g. ● 我不知道他住在哪里。[Wǒ bù zhīdào tā zhù zài nǎlǐ]

I do not know where he lives.

● 我不知道他是中国人。[Wǒ bù zhīdào tā shì Zhōngguó rén]

I do not know he is Chinese.

➢ **Question sentence：subject + 知道[zhīdào] + object + 吗[ma]?**

e.g. ● 你知道那个电影吗？[Nǐ zhīdào nà ge diànyǐng ma]

Do you know that movie?

● 你知道她在哪里工作吗？[Nǐ zhīdào tā zài nǎlǐ gōngzuò ma]

Do you know where she works?

Quiz

I. Pronunciation.

1. Please choose the initials or finals you heard.

1) A. dāo   B. tāo

2) A. gěn   B. kěn

3) A. chāo 　　　　B. zhāo

4) A. gǒu 　　　　B. kǒu

2. Please choose the Pinyin you heard.

1) A. chídào 　　　　B. zhīdào

2) A. zūchē 　　　　B. zuòchē

3) A. chūzū 　　　　B. chūchù

4) A. shēngcí 　　　　B. shéngzi

II. Form sentences.

1. <u>wǒ</u>　　<u>chūzūchē</u>　　<u>tā</u>　　<u>xǐhuan</u>　　<u>zhīdào</u>　　<u>zuò</u>
　　1　　　　2　　　　3　　　4　　　　5　　　　6

2. <u>wǒ</u>　<u>bù</u>　<u>tā</u>　<u>nǎlǐ</u>　<u>zài</u>　<u>zhīdào</u>　<u>zhù</u>
　　1　　2　　3　　4　　5　　　6　　　7

3. <u>zhèlǐ</u>　　<u>wǒ</u>　　<u>zuò</u>　　<u>xǐhuan</u>　　<u>zài</u>
　　1　　　2　　　3　　　4　　　5

4. <u>chūzūchē</u>　　<u>zuò</u>　　<u>qù</u>　　<u>wǒ</u>　　<u>jīchǎng</u>
　　1　　　　2　　　3　　　4　　　5

III. Please translate the following sentences into Chinese.

1. I know what she is called.

2. Do you know where he wants to go?

3. I do not know what it is.

4. I know where can take the taxi.

The Position

Welcome back to our **ChineseAny** podcast series teaching Chinese! This is Level Two, Lesson Twelve. Today we will learn three new words: one noun and two position nouns.

The 1st one, "*fángjiān 房间*", room. "*fáng 房*" is the house, "*jiān 间*" is the room, the room of a house. "*fángjiān 房间*".

For example:

房间
[fángjiān]
room noun

* 我的房间。[Wǒ de fángjiān]
  My room.

* 我的房间在这儿。[Wǒ de fángjiān zài zhèr]
  My room is here.

* 我的房间很好,你的呢? [Wǒ de fángjiān hěn hǎo, nǐ de ne]
  My room is good, how about yours?

OK, the next two position nouns are "*qiánbian 前边*", front and "*hòubian 后边*", back.

前边	后边
[qiánbian]	[hòubian]
front	back

Let's look at a diagram to learn more position nouns in Chinese.

上边 [shàngbian] up	下边 [xiàbian] down

上边 [shàngbian]　　　　下边 [xiàbian]

前边 [qiánbian] front	后边 [hòubian] back

后边 [hòubian]　　　　前边 [qiánbian]

里边 [lǐbian] inside	外边 [wàibian] outside

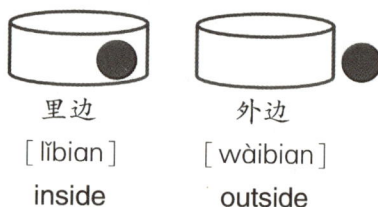

里边 [lǐbian]　　　　外边 [wàibian]
inside　　　　outside

左边 [zuǒbian] left	右边 [yòubian] right

Left　　左边 [zuǒbian]

右边 [yòubian]　　Right

162

旁边
[pángbian]
right by

旁边	附近
[pángbiān]	[fùjìn]
right by	near by

附近
[fùjìn]
near by

北边
[běibian]
north

东边	南边
[dōngbian]	[nánbian]
east	south

西边
[xībian]
west

东边
[dōngbian]
east

西边	北边
[xībian]	[běibian]
west	north

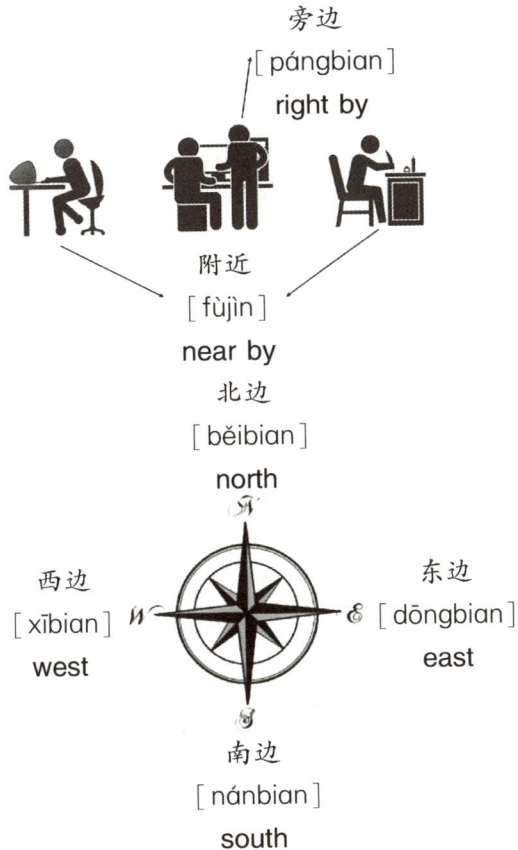

南边
[nánbian]
south

When we would like to express **POSITION or LOCATION**, please remember the following formulas.

① **"A 在** [zài] **some place"**

② **"A 在** [zài] **B 的** [de] **position noun"**

A + 在 + place
[zài]

A + 在 + B 的 + position noun
[zài]　　[de]

③ **Place + 有** [yǒu] **+ sb./ sth.**

④ **B 的** [de] **+ position noun + 有** [yǒu] **+ sb./sth.**

```
place + 有 + Sb./Sth.
        [yǒu]
B 的 + position noun + 有 + Sb./Sth.
[de]                    [yǒu]
```

Let's look at some examples.

● 我在这里。
[Wǒ zài zhèlǐ]
I'm here.

● 妈妈在前边。
[Māma zài qiánbian]
Mom is in the front.

● 面包店在咖啡店左边。
[Miànbāo diàn zài kāfēi diàn de zuǒbian]
The bakery is on the left of the coffee shop.

● 上海在中国的东边。
[Shànghǎi zài Zhōngguó de dōngbian]
Shanghai is in the east of China.

● 他们在房间。
[Tāmen zài fángjiān]
They are in the room.

● 我的家在他的家旁边。
[Wǒ de jiā zài tā de jiā pángbiān]
My home is next to his.

● 我家的前边没有商店。
[Wǒ jiā de qiánbian méiyǒu shāngdiàn]
There is no shop in front of my home.

● 你家的前边有商店吗？
[Nǐ jiā de qiánbian yǒu shāngdiàn ma]
Is there a shop in front of your home?

Great, so that wraps up today's lesson. I hope you have learned something useful about locations in this lesson. Download our app to access our Chinese lessons and learn Chinese anywhere, anytime with **ChineseAny**.

Word List

Main Vocabulary		
房间[fángjiān] room	前边[qiánbian] front	后边[hòubian] back
Additional Vocabulary		
上边[shàngbian] on	下边[xiàbian] under	里边[lǐbian] inside
外边[wàibian] outside	左边[zuǒbian] left	右边[yòubian] right
旁边[pángbiān] beside	附近[fùjìn] nearby	东边[dōngbian] east
西边[xībian] west	南边[nánbian] south	北边[běibian] north

Notes

① **Sentences indicating existence**

➢ **Somebody/something + 在**[Zài] **+ Place**

e. g. ● 我的车在这里。[Wǒ de chē zài zhèlǐ]

My car is here.

- 他们在商店。［Tāmen zài shāngdiàn］

  They are in the shop.

➤ **Place + 有**［yǒu］**+ somebody/something**

e.g. ● 我家有人。［Wǒ jiā yǒu rén］

  There are people in my home.

  ● 商店有东西。［Shāngdiàn yǒu dōngxi］

  There are things in the shop.

➤ **A + 在**［Zài］**+ B 的**［de］**+ location**

e.g. ● 老师在我的前边。［Lǎoshī zài wǒ de qiánbian］

  The teacher is in front of me.

  ● 我家在那个饭店的前边。［Wǒ jiā zài nà ge fàndiàn de qiánbian］

  My home is in front of that restaurant.

➤ **A + location + 有**［yǒu］**+ Somebody/Something**

e.g. ● 咖啡店前边有书店。［Kāfēi diàn qiánbian yǒu shūdiàn］

  There is a book shop in front of the café.

  ● 我家旁边有饭店。［Wǒ jiā pángbiān yǒu fàndiàn］

  There is a restaurant beside my home.

Quiz

I. Pronunciation.

1. Please choose the initials or finals you heard.

  1) A. zhè   B. zè

  2) A. cáng   B. cháng

  3) A. yà   B. yào

  4) A. yuè   B. yùn

2. Please choose the Pinyin you heard.

  1) A. fángjiān   B. fàndiàn

2) A. qiánbian   B. qiántiān

3) A. hòubian   B. hòutiān

4) A. biānmén   B. piānmén

II. Form sentences.

1.
nǐ	zài	zuò	wǒ	kěyǐ	de	qiánbiān
1	2	3	4	5	6	7

2.
qiánbian	chē	méi	fàndiàn	yǒu
1	2	3	4	5

3.
wǒ	zhè	zhù	fángjiān	zài	gè
1	2	3	4	5	6

4.
xǐhuan	tāmen	Hànyǔ	zài	fángjiān	wǒ	xuéxí
1	2	3	4	5	6	7

III. Please translate the following sentences into Chinese.

1. Her room is very nice.

2. I study Chinese in my room.

3. Can I eat dinner in the room?

4. His room is next to my room.

Which One

Welcome to Elementary Level Two, Lesson Thirteen of our **ChineseAny** podcast series teaching Chinese. Today we will learn three new vocabulary words: one pronoun, one measure word and one noun.

The 1st one, "*nǎ 哪*", which.

We normally use "*nǎ 哪 + measure word + noun*" to express "which one".

哪
[nǎ]
which   pronoun

哪 + counting word + noun
[nǎ]
which one

For example:
- 哪个人? [Nǎ gè rén]
  Which person?
- 哪天? [Nǎ tiān]
  Which day?
- 哪国人? [Nǎ guó rén]
  From which country?

Please pay attention to the difference between

"nǎ 哪" and "nǎr 哪儿"; "nǎlǐ 哪里": "nǎ 哪", which; "nǎr 哪儿", "nǎlǐ 哪里" where. We learned "nà 那" is "that" and "nàr 那儿", "there".

哪[nǎ] which(one)	
哪儿[nǎr] where	
‖	
哪里[nǎlǐ] where	

The 2nd character is "běn 本", It's a **measure word** for books, magazines, and notebooks.

本
[běn]
measure word for books

The 3rd word is "shū 书", book. We have already know "diàn 店" means "shop", so "Bookstore" in Chinese is "shūdiàn 书店".

书
[shū]
book　noun

OK, let's make some sentences.
- 这本书 [Zhè běn shū]
  This book.
- 哪本书? [Nǎ běn shū]
  Which book?
- 你喜欢哪个书店? [Nǐ xǐhuan nǎ ge shūdiàn]
  Which bookstore do you like?
- 书店在咖啡店旁边。[Shūdiàn zài kāfēi diàn pángbiān]
  The bookstore is next to the coffee shop.

Great, let's do some exercises to practice what we've learned today.

● 请问，你是哪国人？

[Qǐngwèn, nǐ shì nǎ guó rén]

Excuse me, what nationality are you?

(Where do you come from?)

● 你喜欢哪个？

[Nǐ xǐhuan nǎ ge]

Which one do you like?

● 他是哪个老师的学生？

[Tā shì nǎ ge lǎoshī de xuéshēng]

Which teacher's student is he?

(Who is his teacher?)

● 你要哪个？

[Nǐ yào nǎ gè]

Which one do you want?

● 你想买哪个东西？

[Nǐ xiǎng mǎi nǎ ge dōngxi]

Which thing do you want to buy?

(What do you want to buy?)

● 你们哪天去北京？

[Nǐmen nǎ tiān qù Běijīng]

Which day will you go to Beijing?

(When will you go to Beijing?)

● 哪本书是你的？

[Nǎ běn shū shì nǐ de]

Which book is yours?

● 我喜欢这本书。

[Wǒ xǐhuan zhè běn shū]

I like this book.

Great，so that wraps up today's lesson. Hope you have learned something today. Download our app to access our Chinese lessons. Remember，you can learn Chinese anywhere，anytime with ***ChineseAny***.

◖ Word List

Main Vocabulary		
哪[nǎ] which	本[běn] measure word for books	书[shū] book
Additional Vocabulary		
书店[shūdiàn] bookshop		

◖ Notes

Question mark：哪[nǎ]**which**

哪[nǎ] **+ measure word + objects**

e.g. ● 你喜欢看哪本书？[Nǐ xǐhuan kàn nǎ běn shū]

Which book do you like to read?

- 你要喝哪个咖啡？［Nǐ yào hē nǎ ge kāfēi］
  Which coffee do you want to drink?

- 你们哪天去北京？［Nǐmen nǎ tiān qù Běijīng］
  Which day will you go to Beijing?

- 你哪天去洗车？［Nǐ nǎ tiān qù xǐ chē］
  Which day will you go to wash your car?

Quiz

I. Pronunciation.

  1. Please choose the initials or finals you heard.

    1）A. qiú   B. chú

    2）A. yǎn   B. wǎn

    3）A. lóng   B. nóng

    4）A. jīn   B. jīng

  2. Please choose the Pinyin you heard.

    1）A. shūdiàn   B. shǔtiān

    2）A. kànshū   B. kànchū

    3）A. nàběn   B. nǎběn

    4）A. shìhé   B. chīhē

II. Form sentences.

  1. nǐ   gè   xǐhuan   nǎ   shūdiàn   qù
     1   2   3   4   5   6

  2. nǎ   nǐmen   xuéxí   Hànyǔ   tiān
     1   2   3   4   5

3. nǐ   xiǎng   fàndiàn   qù   nǎ   wǎngshang   gè
   1   2   3   4   5   6   7

4. yào   nǐmen   nǎ   chē   gè   zuò
   1   2   3   4   5   6

III. Please translate the following sentences into Chinese.

1. Which tea do you like to drink?

2. Which book do you want to buy?

3. Which day do you work?

4. Which airport do you want to take?

Can You Help Me

Welcome to Elementary Level Two, Lesson Fourteen of our **ChineseAny** podcast series teaching Chinese. Today we will learn four new vocabulary words: one verb, two counting words, and one number.

The 1st one, "*bāng* 帮", to help.

"*bāng* 帮" means "help somebody to do something". Please be aware that this "help" is not the one you would say when you are in danger.

帮
[bāng]
to help   verb

For example:

- 我帮你。[Wǒ bāng nǐ]
  I will help you.
- 你可以帮我吗? [Nǐ kěyǐ bāng wǒ ma]
  Can you help me?
- 我帮你买东西。[Wǒ bāng nǐ mǎi dōngxi]
  I will help you buy something.

In Chinese, when we would like to express something **in an informal or polite way**, we may REPEAT the verb. If "A" represents a single Chinese verb, we may say "AA", and the second verb should be pronounced in a neutral tone;

"A" → "AA"

For example：

"*kàn 看*" → "*kànkan 看看*"

"*tīng 听*" → "*tīngting 听听*"

"*xiě 写*" → "*xiěxie 写写*"

If the verb is composed of two characters，like "AB"，we may say "ABAB".

"AB" → "ABAB"

For example, we have learned ""*xuéxí 学习*" before, so we may say like this："*xuéxí 学习*" → "*xuéxíxuéxí 学习学习*"

If the verb phrase is composed of a verb (A) + noun (B)，we may say "AAB".

"AB" → "AAB"

For example：

"*kàn shū 看书*" → "*kànkan shū 看看书*"

"*tīng yīnyuè 听音乐*" → "*tīngting yīnyuè 听听音乐*"

"*xiě Hànzi 写汉字*" → "*xiěxie Hànzì 写汉字*"

OK，let see some sentences.

● 我看看。[Wǒ kànkan]

　Let me have a look.

● 我学习学习。[Wǒ xuéxí xuéxí]

　I'd like to learn.

● 我们喝喝咖啡。[wǒmé hē he kāfēi]

　Let's drink some coffee.

● 请帮帮我。[Qǐng bāngbang wǒ]

　Please help me！

　This is more polite and common than 请帮我。[Qǐng bāng wǒ].

The 2nd word, "*yī* 一", means "one",
a **number**.

一
[yī]
One   number

Normally we use it before the **MEASURE
WORD** to express quantity.

We need to change the tone, which shares the same tone rule with
that of "*bù* 不".

"*yī* 一" the 1st tone, as **the single number**, like your phone
number, room number.

"*yí* 一", when there is a "**4th tone**" word after it. For example
"*yí gè* 一个".

"*yì* 一", when there is a "**1st tone**", "**2nd tone**" or a "**3rd tone**"
after it. For example, "*yì tiān* 一天" one day.

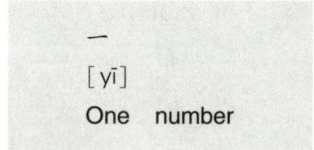

OK, let's look at our two measure words, "*bēi* 杯", cup and "*píng*
瓶", bottle.

For example：

● 一杯水 [yì bēi shuǐ]

One cup of water

"*bēi* 杯" is the 1st tone, so "*yī* 一" needs to change to the 4th
tone.

● 一瓶牛奶 [yì píng niúnǎi]

One bottle of milk

"*píng* 瓶" is the 2nd tone, so "*yī* 一" needs to change to the
4th tone.

OK, let's do some exercises to review and test your understanding
of today's lesson.

- 请帮帮我。

  [Qǐng bāngbang wǒ]

  Please help me.

- 请帮我买一瓶水。

  [Qǐng bāng wǒ mǎi yì píng shuǐ]

  Please help me to buy one bottle of water.

- 你可以帮我买一杯咖啡吗?

  [Nǐ kěyǐ bāng wǒ mǎi yì bēi kāfēi ma]

  Can you help me to buy one cup of coffee?

- 玛姬帮我学习汉语。

  [Mǎjī bāng wǒ xuéxí Hànyǔ]

  Maggie helps me to learn Chinese.

- 今天晚上我可以帮你做饭。

  [Jīntiān wǎnshang wǒ kěyǐ bāng nǐ zuòfàn]

  Tonight I can help you to cook dinner.

- 我可以帮你什么?

  [Wǒ kěyǐ bāng nǐ shénme]

  What can I help you with?

- 哪瓶水是我的?

  [Nǎ píng shuǐ shì wǒ de]

  Which bottle of water is mine?

- 你要哪杯?

  [Nǐ yào nǎ bēi]

  Which cup do you want?

Great, so that wraps up today's lesson. Hope you have learned something. Download our app and learn Chinese anywhere, anytime with **ChineseAny**.

Word List

Main Vocabulary			
帮[bāng] to help	一[yī] one	杯[bēi] cup	瓶[píng] bottle

Notes

① **The repeat of verb：**

> If "A" represents a single Chinese verb, we may say "AA".

　　A —— AA

e.g. ● 你看看这本书。[Nǐ kànkan zhè běn shū]
　　　You have a look at this book.

　　● 你喝喝这瓶水。[Nǐ hēhe zhè píng shuǐ]
　　　You drink this bottle of water.

> If the verb is composed of two characters, like "AB", we may say "ABAB". AB —— ABAB

e.g. ● 今天我们学习学习汉语。[Jīntiān wǒmen xuéxí xuéxí Hànyǔ]
　　　Today we study Chinese.

　　● 他想学习学习这个。[Tā xiǎng xuéxí xuéxí zhège]
　　　He wants to study this.

> If the verb phrase is composed of a verb（A）+noun（B），we

may say "AAB". AB —— AAB

e. g. ● 我们晚上吃吃饭，喝喝咖啡。[Wǒmen wǎnshang chīchi fàn, hēhe kāfēi]

We can eat food, drink coffee in the evening.

● 他们喜欢看看电影，听听音乐。[Tāmen xǐhuan kànkan diànyǐng，tīngting yīnyuè]

They like to watch a movie, and listen to music.

Quiz

I. Pronunciation.

1. Please choose the initials or finals you heard.

1) A. dài   B. tài

2) A. lán   B. nán

3) A. dōu   B. duō

4) A. yǎo   B. yǒu

2. Please choose the Pinyin you heard.

1) A. bànfǎ   B. bānfā

2) A. bǎibù   B. běibù

3) A. mǎi shuǐ   B. mài shuǐ

4) A. gòu le   B. gào le

II. Form sentences.

1. <u>qǐng</u>   <u>mǎi</u>   <u>píng</u>   <u>bāng</u>   <u>wǒ</u>   <u>shuǐ</u>   <u>yì</u>
   1   2   3   4   5   6   7

2. <u>wǒ</u>   <u>bāng</u>   <u>Hànyǔ</u>   <u>Sophie</u>   <u>xuéxí</u>
   1   2   3   4   5

3. bēi   wǒ   gè   zhōng   yào   yì   nátiě (Latte)
   1   2   3   4   5   6   7

---

4. nǐ   nǎ   xiǎng   bēi   yào
   1   2   3   4   5

III. Please translate the following sentences into Chinese.

1. What can I help you?

_____

2. I can help you to cook Chinese food.

_____

3. Could you help me to buy a Chinese book?

_____

4. She cannot help me to study Chinese.

_____

Please Come in

Welcome back to our **ChineseAny** podcast series teaching Chinese. This is Elementary Level Two, Lesson Fifteen. Today we will learn three new words: one noun, one adverb, and one verb. Let's start our lesson.

The 1st one is a noun, "*piào* 票", ticket.

票
[piào]
Ticket   noun

For example:
- 电影票 [diànyǐng piào]
  movie ticket
- 买票 [mǎi piào]
  to buy the ticket
- 有票 [yǒu piào]
  have a ticket
- 没有票 [méiyǒu piào]
  there is no ticket

Previously, we learned "*jīchǎng* 机场", airport. Here "*jī* 机" means "airplane", so could you tell me how you would say "airplane ticket" in Chinese? Great, that is "*jīpiào* 机票".

And we learned that "car" in Chinese is "*chē* 车", so "*chēpiào* 车票" can be used to express "train, subway, or bus ticket".

OK, let's look at the 2nd adverb, "*tài . . . le* 太……了", which means "too . . ." We usually put an **ADJECTIVE** between it,

太……了
[tài . . . le]
too   adverb

For example,

- 太好了 [Tài hǎo le]
  it's too good!
- 我太累了。[Wǒ tài lèi le]
  I'm too tired.
- 那个咖啡太难喝了。[Nà ge kāfēi tài nánhē le]
  That coffee is too hard to drink.

You can now put all of the adjectives you've learned to practice and to test your comprehension of this new adverb.

When you would like to give the negative meaning, you may say "*bú tài* 不太…", which means "it's not very . . .". Please pay attention, here there is no "*le* 了" anymore.

不太……
[bú tài]
not very + adjective

For example,

- 我的汉语不太好。[Wǒ de Hànyǔ bú tài hǎo]
  My Chinese is not very good.
- 今天我不太忙。[Jīntiān wǒ bú tài máng]
  Today I'm not very busy.

The 3rd character is a verb, "*jìn* 进" "*jìn* 进" means "to enter, to come in".

进
[jìn]
to enter   verb

For example,

- 请进！[Qǐng jìn]

  Please come in!

- 请进我的房间。[Qǐng jìn wǒ de fángjiān]

  Please come in to my room.

- 你不可以进这个房间。[Nǐ bù kěyǐ jìn zhège fángjiān]

  You cannot enter this room.

I hope you remember the antonym of "*jìn* 进".

When we learned "*chūzū chē* 出租车", taxi, I told you "*chū* 出" means "out". So "*jìn* 进" is "come in", "*chū* 出" is "go out".

进	≠	出
[jìn]		[chū]
come in		go out

Great, let's do some exercises to review and test your comprehension of today's lesson.

- 我去买电影票。

  [Wǒ qù mǎi diànyǐng piào]

  I will go to buy movie tickets.

- 你有票吗?

  [Nǐ yǒu piào ma]

  Do you have the tickets?

- 我可以进你的房间看看吗?

  [Wǒ kěyǐ jìn nǐ de fángjiān kànkan ma]

  Can I enter your room to have a look?

- 请进,请坐!

  [Qǐng jìn, qǐng zuò]

  Please come in and sit down.

- 你想买什么票?

  [Nǐ xiǎng mǎi shénme piào]

  What ticket do you want to buy?

- 没有车票不可以坐车。

  [Méiyǒu chēpiào bù kěyǐ zuò chē]

  You cannot take train without a ticket.

- 这里也可以买机票。

  [Zhèlǐ yě kěyǐ mǎi jīpiào]

  Here you can also buy the airplane tickets.

Great, so that wraps up today's lesson. Hope you have learned something. You can download our app to access all of our Chinese lessons and learn Chinese anywhere, anytime with *ChineseAny*.

Word List

Main Vocabulary		
票 [piào] ticket	太 [tài] too	进 [jìn] to enter
Additional Vocabulary		
电影票 [diànyǐng piào] movie ticket	机票 [jīpiào] air ticket	车票 [chēpiào] bus ticket

Notes

① **Degree adjective：太** [tài] ······ **了** [le]

太[tài] **+ adjective +** (了[le])

The negative form of "太[tài]**" is "**不太[bú tài]**".**

e. g. ● 这个电影太好看了。[Zhège diànyǐng tài hǎokàn le]

That movie is too nice.

● 他太太太好了。[Tā tàitài tài hǎo le]

His wife is too good.

● 我今天不太累。[Wǒ jīntiān bú tài lèi]

I am not too tired today.

● 他们明天不太忙。[Tāmen míngtiān bú tài máng]

They are not too busy tomorrow.

Q **Quiz**

I. Pronunciation.

1. Please choose the initials or finals you heard.

1) A. zī B. cī

2) A. fēng B. bēng

3) A. yōu B. jiū

4) A. wǎn B. wǎng

2. Please choose the Pinyin you heard.

1) A. diànyǐng B. gǎnyìng

2) A. jīpiào B. jǐ tiáo

3) A. jìn lái B. qǐng lái

4) A. tài féi B. tài hēi

II. Form sentences.

1. <u>nǐ</u>　<u>mǎi</u>　<u>nǎ ge</u>　<u>xiǎng</u>　<u>diànyǐng</u>　<u>piào</u>
　　1　　2　　3　　4　　5　　6

2. le   zhège   tài   hǎo chī   fàn
1   2   3   4   5

_____

3. yǒu   piào   ma   nǐ   diànyǐng
1   2   3   4   5

_____

4. máng   gōngzuò   bú   wǒ de   tài
1   2   3   4   5

_____

III. Please translate the following sentences into Chinese.

1. I am too busy today, how about you?

_____

2. I can help you to buy the air ticket.

_____

3. The Chinese tea is too tasty.

_____

4. Could I enter her room?

_____

How Much Is It

Welcome to Elementary Level Two, Lesson Sixteen of our **ChineseAny** podcast series teaching Chinese. Today we will learn three new words: one special question word, one noun, and one adjective. Let's look at them now.

The 1st one, "*duōshao* 多少", "how much".

"*duō* 多" means "much, many". You may say "*hěn duō* 很多", "very much"; "*bù duō* 不多", "not much, not many".

多少
[duōshao]
How many, how much
Special question word

We can use "*hěn duō* 很多" in the following situation:
"*hěn duō* 很多" + **NOUN**,

For example,

- 很多朋友 [Hěn duō péngyou]
  many friends
- 很多人 [Hěn duō rén]
  many people
- 很多牛奶 [Hěn duō niúnǎi]
  a lot of milk

You may try to put all the nouns you have learned after "*hěn duō* 很多" to practice this structure.

Great, let's see the "*shǎo* 少". "*shǎo* 少" means "little, few".

You may say "*hěn shǎo* 很少", "very few, very little"；"*bù shǎo* 不少"means "not few, not a little" and it also means "very much"！You usually use it before nouns.

So "*duōshao* 多少" means "how much". We usually use in the following patterns：

① **duōshao 多少 + measure word + noun**?

② **duōshao 多少 + qián 钱**? How much money?

The 2nd character is "*qián* 钱". It means "money".

> 钱
> [qián]
> money   noun

For example,

● 这个多少钱? [Zhè ge duōshao qián]
How much is this?

● 这瓶啤酒多少钱? [Zhè píng píjiǔ duōshao qián]
How much is this bottle of beer?

● 一杯咖啡多少钱? [Yì bēi kāfēi duōshao qián]
How much is one cup of coffee?

● 他有很多钱。[Tā yǒu hěn duō qián]
He has a lot of money.

● 我没有钱。[Wǒ méiyǒu qián]
I have no money.

Can you guess how to say "rich person" in Chinese? "Rich person also translates to **have money person**", Yes, that is "*yǒu qián rén* 有钱人",

For example,

- 他是有钱人。[Tā shì yǒuqián rén]

  He is a rich man.

- 我爸爸不是有钱人。[Wǒ bàba bú shì yǒuqián rén]

  My father is not a rich man.

Great, let's see our 3rd character, "*guì* 贵*", "expensive". It's an adjective.

贵

[guì]

expensive   adverb

For example,

- 有点儿贵 [yǒudiǎnr guì]

  a little bit expensive

- 很贵 [hěn guì]

  very expensive

- 不贵 [bú guì]

  not expensive

Great, let's do some exercises to review and understand what we learned today.

- 你有多少中国朋友?

  [Nǐ yǒu duōshao Zhōngguó péngyou]

  How many Chinese friends do you have?

- 你可以喝多少瓶啤酒?

  [Nǐ kěyǐ hē duōshao píng píjiǔ]

  How many bottles of beer can you drink?

● 今天晚上来多少人？

[Jīntiān wǎnshang lái duōshao rén]

How many people will come tonight?

● 你知道多少个汉字？

[Nǐ zhīdào duōshao ge Hànzì]

How many characters do you know?

● 明天我要买很多东西。

[Míngtiān wǒ yào mǎi hěn duō dōngxi]

Tomorrow I shall need to buy many things.

● 我们都不是有钱人。

[Wǒmen dōu bú shì yǒuqián rén]

None of us are rich people.

● 那里中国人很少。

[Nàlǐ Zhōngguó rén hěn shǎo]

There are few Chinese people there.

Great, so that wraps up today's lesson. I hope you have learned something there. Download our **ChineseAny** app to access our Chinese lessons and learn Chinese anywhere, anytime.

Word List

Main Vocabulary		
多少[duōshao] how many	钱[qián] money	贵[guì] expensive

Additional Vocabulary		
多 [duō] many	少 [shǎo] few	有钱人 [yǒuqián rén] rich person

Notes

① **"how many" question sentence**：

➤ **多少** [duōshao] **+ measure word + noun**?

e. g. ● 你有多少汉语老师? [Nǐ yǒu duōshao Hànyǔ lǎoshī]

How many Chinese teachers do you have?

● 他们要买多少书? [Tāmen yào mǎi duōshao shū]

How many books do they want to buy?

➤ **多少** [duōshao] **+ 钱** [qián]?

e. g. ● 一瓶啤酒多少钱? [Yì píng píjiǔ duōshao qián]

How much is a bottle of beer?

● 一本汉语书多少钱? [Yì běn Hànyǔ shū duōshao qián]

How much is a Chinese book?

Quiz

I. Pronunciation.

1. Please choose the initials or finals you heard.

1) A. rè   B. lè

2) A. shuō   B. suō

3) A. jūn   B. qún

4) A. bīn   B. bīng

2. Please choose the Pinyin you heard.

1) A. hěn shǎo   B. hěn chǎo

2) A. tài guì   B. tài kuī

3) A. yǒuxiàn   B. yǒu qián

4) A. duō chī   B. tuōchē

II. Form sentences.

1. <u>Zhōngguó</u> <u>duōshao</u> <u>yǒu</u> <u>rén</u>
 1   2   3   4

_____

2. <u>Zhè ge</u> <u>duōshao</u> <u>dōngxi</u> <u>qián</u>
 1   2   3   4

_____

3. <u>guì</u> <u>le</u> <u>jīpiào</u> <u>tài</u>
 1 2 3   4

_____

4. <u>tā de</u> <u>hěn</u> <u>péngyou</u> <u>duō</u>
 1   2   3   4

_____

III. Please translate the following sentences into Chinese.

1. She has a lot of Chinese books.

_____

2. How much is this movie ticket?

_____

3. That thing is too expensive; I do not want to buy.

_____

4. I think he has a lot of money.

_____

Numbers

Welcome to Elementary Level Two, Lesson Seventeen of our **ChineseAny** podcast series teaching Chinese. Today we will learn numbers. Let's look at them now.

Zero to ten is：

零 ［líng］	Zero	
一 ［yī］	One	

二 ［èr］	Two	
三 ［sān］	Three	

四 ［sì］	Four	
五 ［wǔ］	Five	

六 ［liù］	Six	
七 ［qī］	Seven	

八 ［bā］	Eight	
九 ［jiǔ］	Nine	

十 ［shí］	Ten

In Chinese, we use them for room number, phone number and all kinds of "numbers".

号码
［hàomǎ］
number　noun

So the 2nd vocabulary is "*hàomǎ* 号码", "number".

For example：

- 房间号码[fángjiān hàomǎ]
  Room number
- 我在 1208 房间。[Wǒ zài yī èr líng bā fángjiān]
  I'm in Room 1208.
- 我的房间号码是 4302。[Wǒ de fángjiān hàomǎ shì sì sān líng èr]
  My Room number is 4302.

When we ask the number, you may use "what —*shénme* 什么" or "how many —*duōshao* 多少".

For example：

"What's your room number? "

① "*Nǐ de fángjiān hàomǎ shì shénme* 你的房间号码是什么？ "

② "*Nǐ de fángjiān hàomǎ shì duōshao* 你的房间号码是多少？ "

There are some points we need to pay attention to when we use numbers.

① When we use "*yī* 一" to express the phone number, room number or other numbers，normally we change the pronunciation to "*yāo* 一" to make it clearer to the listener. For example, if the number is 1111，"*yī yī yī yī* " can be hard to hear clearly, but "*yāo yāo yāo yāo* " is much better, right?

For example：

- 我在 1208 房间。[Wǒ zài yī èr líng bā fángjiān]
- 我在 1208 房间。[Wǒ zài yāo èr líng bā fángjiān]

Which one is easier to understand? I think the 2nd one, how about you?

② When we use "*èr* 二" with a measure word after it，we need to change it to "*liǎng* 两".

For example,

- "two cups of coffee" cannot be "*èr bēi kāfēi* 二杯咖啡", but "*liǎng bēi kāfēi* 两杯咖啡".

The same is true for

- 两瓶水 [Liǎng píng shuǐ]
  Two bottles of water
- 两本书 [Liǎng běn shū]
  Two books
- "Two persons", "*Liǎng gè rén* 两个人", but not "*èr* 二".

Please remember "*èr* 二" is only used in expressing an actual number but not a quantity.

③ Chinese people always use body language to express the numbers. Please follow your teacher to read them aloud and perform the gestures.

④ Regarding numbers bigger than TEN：

For multiples of ten，we just need to put the number before the ten to express it.

10 十 Ten [shí]	2 +10 二十 Twenty [èr shí]
3 +10 三十 Thirty [sān shí]	4 +10 四十 Forty [sì shí]
5 +10 五十 Fifty [wǔ shí]	6 +10 六十 Sixty [liù shí]
7 +10 七十 Seventy [qī shí]	8 +10 八十 Eighty [bā shí]

9 + 10	九十
Ninety	[jiǔ shí]

For 11 – 19, we just need to put the numbers after the ten.

10	十
Ten	[shí]

10 + 1	十一
Eleven	[shíyī]

10 + 2	十二
Twelve	[shíèr]

10 + 3	十三
Thirteen	[shísān]

10 + 4	十四
Fourteen	[shísì]

10 + 5	十五
Fifteen	[shíwǔ]

10 + 6	十六
Sixteen	[shíliù]

10 + 7	十七
Seventeen	[shíqī]

10 + 8	十八
Eighteen	[shíbā]

10 + 9	十九
Nineteen	[shíjiǔ]

The same rule is for "21 – 29, 31 – 29 to 91 – 99", You may try it by yourselves. If you have any question, please leave a message to our teachers.

Great, so that wraps up today's lesson. Hope you have learned something useful. Download our app to access our Chinese lessons. Remember, you can learn Chinese anywhere, anytime with **ChineseAny**.

◯ **Word List**

Main Vocabulary		
零[líng] zero	一[yī] one	二[èr] two
三[sān] three	四[sì] four	五[wǔ] five
六[liù] six	七[qī] seven	八[bā] eight
九[jiǔ] nine	十[shí] ten	号码[hàomǎ] number
Additional Vocabulary		
一[yāo] one	两[liǎng] two	十一[shíyī] eleven
十二[shíèr] twelve	十三[shísān] thirteen	十四[shísì] fourteen
十五[shíwǔ] fifteen	十六[shíliù] sixteen	十七[shíqī] seventeen
十八[shíbā] eighteen	十九[shíjiǔ] nineteen	二十[èrshí] twenty
三十[sānshí] thirty	四十[sìshí] forty	五十[wǔshí] fifty
六十[liùshí] sixty	七十[qīshí] seventy	八十[bāshí] eighty
九十[jiǔshí] ninety		

○ **Notes**

The difference between "二[èr]" and "两[liǎng]"

When we use "二[èr]" with a counting word after it, we need to change it to "两[liǎng]". Please remember "二[èr]" is only used in expressing an actual number but not a quantity.

e.g. ● 两杯茶 [liǎng bēi chá]

　　　Two cups of tea

　　● 两个中国人 [liǎng ge Zhōngguó rén]

　　　Two Chinese people

　　● 两瓶啤酒 [liǎng píng píjiǔ]

　　　Two bottles of beer

○ **Quiz**

I. Pronunciation.

　1. Please choose the initials or finals you heard.

　　　1) A. gāi　　　　　　　　B. kāi

　　　2) A. hē　　　　　　　　B. gē

　　　3) A. niáng　　　　　　　B. liáng

　　　4) A. hǎo　　　　　　　　B. hǒu

　2. Please choose the Pinyin you heard.

　　　1) A. shí sì　　　　　　　B. sì shí

　　　2) A. bù xiǎo　　　　　　　B. bù shǎo

　　　3) A. diànnǎo　　　　　　　B. diànnià n

　　　4) A. liángkuai　　　　　　　B. liǎng kuài

II. Form sentences.

1. <u>wǔ</u>   <u>líng</u>   <u>zhù</u>   <u>èr</u>   <u>fángjiān</u>   <u>wǒmen</u>
   1   2   3   4   5   6

_____

2. <u>qǐng</u>   <u>wǒ</u>   <u>mǎi</u>   <u>bāng</u>   <u>liǎng gè</u>   <u>diànnǎo</u>
   1   2   3   4   5   6

_____

3. <u>liǎng</u>   <u>nàlǐ</u>   <u>gè</u>   <u>yǒu</u>   <u>fàngdiàn</u>
   1   2   3   4   5

_____

4. <u>yǒu</u>   <u>gè</u>   <u>fǎngjiān</u>   <u>xuésheng</u>   <u>lǐ</u>   <u>sānshí</u>   <u>zài</u>
   1   2   3   4   5   6   7

_____

III. Please translate the following sentences into Chinese.

1. He has two jobs.

_____

2. They have two Chinese teachers.

_____

3. How much are two bottles of milk?

_____

4. — Which room do you live in?
   — Room 612.

_____

Cheaper, Please

Welcome to Elementary Level Two, Lesson Eighteen of our **ChineseAny** podcast series teaching Chinese. Today we will learn about the Chinese currency units or RMB, one adjective, and one grammar point. Let's start our lesson now.

We have learned money and numbers in Chinese. The 1st noun is "*qián* 钱". Today let's learn the units of Chinese RMB.

钱
[qián]
money   noun

There are 3 units for Chinese RMB, they are：

- "*yuán* 元 = *kuài* 块"
  "*yuán* 元" is formal form and "*kuài* 块" is informal form.
- "*Jiǎo* 角 = *máo* 毛"
  "*Jiǎo* 角" is formal form and "*máo* 毛" is informal form.
- "*Fēn* 分" is informal form and Formal form

In Chinese we say：

1 yuán shì 10 jiǎo，一元是十角,*1 Yuan is 10 jiao.*

1 jiǎo shì 10 fēn，一角是十分,*1 jiao is 10 cents.*

For example，

- 1.5RMB shì *1 yuán 5 jiǎo*. Verbally, you may also say "*1 kuài 5 máo* 一块五毛".

Let's try to express the following amounts in Chinese. Please be aware that the last unit of the amount can be omitted.

For example,

- "20.6RMB" =20 元 6 角 [er shi yuán liu jiǎo]

    20 块 6 毛 [ershi kuài liu máo]

- "16RMB" =16 元 [yuán]

    16 块 [kuài]

- "50.55RMB" =50 元 5 角 5 分 [wushi yuán wu jiǎo wu fēn]

    50 块 5 毛 5 分 [Wushi kuài wu máo wu fēn]

The 2nd word is an adjective, "*piányi*
便宜". It means "cheap".

> 便宜
> [piányi]
> cheap   adjective

You may say

- 很便宜 [hěn piányi]

    very cheap

- 太便宜了 [tài piányi le]

    too cheap

- 不便宜 [bù piányi]

    not cheap

In Lesson 16, we've learned its antonym "*guì* 贵", "expensive".

At the end of our lesson, we will learn one grammar point, how to express the "Comparative degree" in Chinese. The Comparative Degree is the comparative form of an adjective or adverb. For example, "faster" is the comparative of the adjective "fast" or "less famous" is the comparative of "famous". In Chinese, we normally put the "*yìdiǎnr*
一点儿" after the Adjective to form the "Comparative degree".

For example,

- 很贵 [Hěn guì]
  very expensive
- 便宜一点儿 [Piányi yìdiǎnr]
  cheaper
- 很难吃 [Hěn nánchī]
  very hard to eat (It tastes terrible.)
- 好吃一点儿 [Hǎochī yìdiǎnr]
  more delicious
- 很早 [hěn zǎo]
  very early
- 晚一点儿 [wǎn yìdiǎnr]
  later

Great, let's do some exercises to practice what we have learned from today's lesson.

- 这个多少钱？
  [Zhè ge duōshao qián]
  How much is this?

- 25 RMB.
  [Èrshíwǔ kuài]
  25 RMB.

- 太贵了，可以便宜一点儿吗？
  [Tài guì le, kěyǐ piányi yìdiǎnr ma]
  It's too expensive, can it be cheaper?

- 对不起，不可以。
  [Duì bu qǐ, bù kěyǐ]
  Sorry.

Great, so that wraps up today's lesson. Congratulations! This is the last lesson of the Level Two course. You've come a long way and I hope you've learned something useful. Now that you have completed this level, please be sure to check out our practice library to test what you have learned in this level. Download our app to access our Chinese lessons. As always, you can learn Chinese anywhere, anytime with **ChineseAny**.

Word List

Main Vocabulary		
元[yuán] yuan (the basic of monetary of China	角[jiǎo] jiao (the fractional monetary of unit of China, =1/10 of a yuan)	便宜[piányi] cheap
Additional Vocabulary		
块[kuài] kuai (the basic of monetary of China)	毛[máo] mao (the fractional monetary of unit of China, =1/10 of a yuan)	分[fēn] fen (the fractional monetary of unit of China, =1/10 of a jiao)

Notes

Adjective + 一点儿[yìdiǎnr], **Comparative degree.**

e.g. ● 这个好一点儿。[Zhè ge hǎo yìdiǎnr]
This is a little better.

● 可以便宜一点儿吗?[Kěyǐ piányi yìdiǎnr ma]
Could it be a little cheaper?

● 这个好喝一点儿。[Zhè ge hǎohē yìdiǎnr]
This is a little better to drink. (It tastes better.)

● 他的朋友多一点儿。[Tā de péngyou duō yìdiǎnr]
He has a little bit more friends. (He has more friends.)

Quiz

I. Pronunciation.

  1. Please choose the initials or finals you heard.

    1) A. bái   B. pái

    2) A. zāng   B. zān

    3) A. qǐ   B. xǐ

    4) A. jiǎo   B. qiǎo

  2. Please choose the Pinyin you heard.

    1) A. piányi   B. biànyì

    2) A. túdì   B. tǔdì

    3) A. jiǎoluò   B. qiāo luó

    4) A. fāngbiàn   B. fángjiān

II. Form sentences.

1.
yì	sānshíyī	kuài	kāfēi	bēi
1	2	3	4	5

2.
shuǐguǒ	piányi	kěyǐ	ma	yìdiǎn	nǐ de
1	2	3	4	5	6

3.
zài	shū	Zhōngguó	hěn	piányi	mǎi
1	2	3	4	5	6

4.
kěyǐ	xǐ	zhèlǐ	shǒu	ma
1	2	3	4	5

III. Please translate the following sentences into Chinese.

1. I want to drink some water.

_____

2. It is too expensive, please a little cheaper.

_____

3. She is too busy; she cannot cook in this evening.

_____

4. A bottle of water costs two dollars.

_____

三

级

These and Those

Welcome to Elementary Level Three, Lesson One of our **ChineseAny** podcast series teaching Mandarin Chinese. Today we will learn three words, one pronoun, one measure word, and one noun. Let's start our lesson now.

In our previous lessons, we learned "*zhègè* 这个", "this one"; "*nàgè* 那个" "that one", and "*yígè* 一个", "one".

Today, let's learn their plural forms. All we need to do is put "*xiē* 些" after them.

> 些
> [xiē]
> plural form of this or that

"*zhègè* 这个" changes to "*zhèxiē* 这些", "these".
"*nàgè* 那个" changes to "*nàxiē* 那些", "those".
"*yígè* 一个" changes to "*yìxiē* 一些", "some".

"*zhèxiē rén* 这些人", "these people".
"*zhèxiē dōngxi* 这些东西", "these things".
"*nàxiē hànzì* 那些汉字", "those Chinese characters".
"*nàxiē rén* 那些人", "those people".

You can also put measure words and a noun after them.
- "*zhè bēi kāfēi* 这杯咖啡", this cup of coffee, the plural form is

"*zhèxiē bēi kāfēi* 这些杯咖啡", these cups of coffee.

- "*nà píng píjiǔ* 那瓶啤酒", that bottle of beer, the plural form is "*nàxiē píng píjiǔ* 那些瓶啤酒", those bottles of beer.

OK, let's look at the 2nd word, "*jīn* 斤". It's a measure word, which means "500 grams".

斤
[jīn]
500 grams   measure word

In China, we normally measure weight by units of 500 grams. "*yì jīn* 一斤" is 500 grams, "*liǎng jīn* 两斤" is 1 000 grams.

一斤 = 500 grams
两斤 = 1,000 grams

For example：

- 我想买两斤水果。[Wǒ xiǎng mǎi liǎng jīn shuǐguǒ]
  I want to buy 2 *jin* fruits.
- 水果多少钱一斤？[Shuǐguǒ duōshǎo qián yì jīn]
  How much per *jin* of these fruits?

You may also use other counting words when asking for the price of something.

For example：

- 汉语书多少钱一本？
  [Hànyǔ shū duōshǎo qián yì běn]
  How much for one copy of the Chinese book?

- 45 块钱一本。
  [Sìshí wǔ kuài qián yì běn]
  45 yuan for one copy.

● 咖啡多少钱一杯?
［Kāfēi duōshǎo qián yì bēi］
How much for one cup of coffee?

● 31 块钱一杯。
［Sān shí yī kuài qián yì bēi］
31 yuan for one cup.

OK，let's move to today's 3rd character，
"*cài* 菜"，which means "vegetables or dish".

Chinese people usually have "*fàn* 饭"，rice
and "*cài* 菜" together for a meal.

菜
［cài］
vegetables   noun

You can say "*Zhōngguó cài* 中国菜" for Chinese food，"*Fǎguó cài*
法国菜" for French food.

So can you tell me 你喜欢吃什么菜? ［Nǐ xǐhuān chī shénme cài］
What dish do you like to eat?

Great，let's do some exercises to review what we learned today.

● 这些菜多少斤?
［Zhè xiē cài duōshǎo jīn］
How many grams are these vegetables?

● 这些电影都很好看。
［Zhè xiē diànyǐng dōu hěn hǎokàn］
These movies are all nice（great）.

● 我有一些中国朋友。
[Wǒ yǒu yì xiē Zhōngguó péngyǒu]
I have some Chinese friends.

● 那些书是我的。
[Nà xiē shū shì wǒ de]
Those books are mine.

● 妈妈做菜很好吃。
[Māma zuò cài hěn hǎochī]
My mom can cook well.

● 今天的饭菜很好吃。
[Jīntiān de fàncài hěn hǎochī]
Today's food is very delicious.

Great, so that wraps up today's lesson. Hope have you learned something there. Download our app to access our Chinese lessons. Remember, you can learn Chinese anywhere, anytime with **ChineseAny**.

Word List

Main Vocabulary		
这些[zhèxiē] these	斤[jīn] half kilogram	菜[cài] dish, vegetables
Additional Vocabulary		
些[xiē] some	那些[nàxiē] those	一些[yìxiē] some

◯ **Notes**

多少钱 [Duōshao qián]：**How much**?

Noun + **多少钱** [duōshao qián] + **一** [yī] + **measure words** —
asking for the price of something.

e. g. ● 水果多少钱一斤? [Shuǐguǒ duōshao qián yì jīn]

How much per jin of these fruits?

● 咖啡多少钱一杯? [Kāfēi duōshao qián yì bēi]

How much for a cup of coffee?

◯ **Quiz**

I. Pronunciation.

1. Please choose the initials or finals you heard.

　　1) A. yuè　　　　　　　B. yù

　　2) A. lín　　　　　　　B. líng

　　3) A. hǎo　　　　　　　B. kǎo

　　4) A. cān　　　　　　　B. chān

2. Please choose the Pinyin you heard.

　　1) A. míngtiān　　　　　B. měitiān

　　2) A. duōshao　　　　　B. dōu shǎo

　　3) A. nǎxiē　　　　　　B. nàxiē

　　4) A. yìjīn　　　　　　B. yǐjīng

II. Form sentences.

1. <u>jīn</u>   <u>píngguǒ</u>   <u>duōshao</u>   <u>qián</u>   <u>yì</u>
     1   2   3   4   5

   _____

2. <u>cài</u>   <u>nǐ</u>   <u>chī</u>   <u>shénme</u>   <u>xīhuan</u>
     1   2   3   4   5

   _____

3. <u>nàxiē</u>   <u>shì</u>   <u>rén</u>   <u>lǎoshī</u>   <u>dōu</u>
     1   2   3   4   5

   _____

4. <u>yìxiē</u>   <u>yǒu</u>   <u>Hànyǔ</u>   <u>wǒ</u>   <u>shū</u>
     1   2   3   4   5

   _____

III. Please translate the following sentences into Chinese.

1. I want to buy two pounds of apple.

   _____

2. These are not right; you can go to ask your teacher.

   _____

3. I have some Chinese friends.

   _____

4. Those dishes are not delicious.

   _____

This Year

Welcome to Elementary Level Three, Lesson Two of our **ChineseAny** podcast series teaching Mandarin Chinese. Today we will learn three time-related words.

They are:

"*nián* 年", year.

> 年
> [nián]
> year　noun

"*yuè* 月", month.

> 月
> [yuè]
> month　noun

"*rì* 日", date. We also say "*hào* 号" verbally.

> 日　　号
> [rì]　　[hào]
> verbally　noun

In Chinese, we usually express the date from the longer unit of time to the shorter one.

So "Today is 10th Feb, 2015" in Chinese should be "*Jīntiān shì*

2015 nián èr yuè shí rì（hào） 今天是2015 年2 月10 日（号）".

2015	Year	2	Month	10	Date
2015	年	二	月	十	日（号）
[2015	nián	èr	yuè	shí	rì（hào）]

● "One year" is "*yì nián* 一年". Please pay attention to that there is no counting word for "*nián* 年".

● "One month" is "*yí gè yuè* 一个月", "*gè* 个" is the measure word for "*yuè* 月".

● "one day" should be "*yì tiān* 一天", not "*yī rì* 一日" or "*yī hào* 一号". "*tiān* 天" means "day", but "*yī rì* 一日" or "*yī hào* 一号" means "date one".

OK, let's learn something else. Before, we learned "*jīntiān* 今天" for today, this day. "*míngtiān* 明天" for tomorrow, next day.

So "this year" in Chinese would be "*jīnnián* 今年", "next year" is "*míngnián* 明年".

Previously we learned "*qián* 前", which means "before". So "the year before last year" in Chinese is "*qiánnián* 前年". "The year after the next year", which in Chinese should be "*hòu nián* 后年".

So, "*jīnnián* 今年", "*míngnián* 明年", "*qiánnián* 前年", "*hòu nián* 后年" are the additional vocabularies for this lesson, please pay attention to them.

Let's see some examples：

● 今年是 2015 年。[Jīnnián shì 2015 nián]

   This year is 2015.

● 明年是 2016 年。[Míngnián shì 2016 nián]

Next year is 2016.

- 今天是 7 月 9 号。[Jīntiān shì 7 yuè 9 hào]
Today is 9th July.
- 明天是 7 月 10 号。[Míngtiān shì 7 yuè 10 hào]
Tomorrow is 10th July.

Did you see the difference between
"*yī yuè* 一月" and "*yí gè yuè* 一个月"?
Yes, without the measure word, "*yī yuè* 一月" means "January". "*yīgèyuè* 一个月" means "one month". Please pay attention to that.

一月	一个月
[yī yuè]	[yíge yuè]
January	one month

Now, please read and review the names of the months in Chinese.

一月 [yī yuè] January	二月 [èr yuè] February
三月 [sān yuè] March	四月 [sì yuè] April
五月 [wǔ yuè] May	六月 [liù yuè] June
七月 [qī yuè] July	八月 [bā yuè] August

九月　　［jiǔ yuè］
September

十月　　［shí yuè］
October

十一月　　［shíyī yuè］
November

十二月　　［shíèr yuè］
December

Great，let's do some exercises to review what we have learned today.

● 一月一号我去北京。
　　［yī yuè yī hào wǒ qù Běijīng］
I will go to Beijing on Jan 1st.

● 他要在这里住一年。
　　［Tā yào zài zhèlǐ zhù yì nián］
He will live here for one year.

● 六月我很忙。
　　［Liùyuè wǒ hěn máng］
I will be busy in June.

● 今年八月我不去上海。
　　［Jīnnián bāyuè wǒ bú qù Shànghǎi］
I will not go to Shanghai this August.

- 一年有多少个月？

  [Yì nián yǒu duōshǎo ge yuè]

  How many months are there in one year?

- 这个月有多少天？

  [Zhège yuè yǒu duōshǎo tiān]

  How many days are there in this month?

- 明年我要去北京看朋友。

  [Míngnián wǒ yào qù Běijīng kàn péngyǒu]

  I will go to Beijing to see my friends next year.

- 明年九月我不在中国。

  [Míngnián jiǔyuè wǒ bú zài Zhōngguó]

  I will not be in China next September.

Great, so that wraps up today's lesson. Hope you have learned something there. Download our app to access our Chinese lessons and learn Chinese anywhere, anytime with **ChineseAny**.

Word List

Main Vocabulary		
年[nián] year	月[yuè] month	日[rì]\号[hào] date
Additional Vocabulary		
今年[jīnnián] this year	明年[míngnián] next year	前年[qiánnián] the year before last year
后年[hòunián] the year after next year		

Notes

① 年[nián]**year,** 月[yuè]**month &** 日\号[rì]\[hào]**date：**

e.g. ● 今天是2015年2月10日(号)。[Jīntiān shì èr líng yī wǔ nián èr yuè shí rì(hào)]

Today is 10th Feb, 2015.

● 二零零八年十月一号[èr líng líng bā nián shí yuè yī hào]

01/10/2008

② 年[nián]**year,** 月[yuè]**month &** 日\天[rì]\[tiān]

一个月[yí gè yuè]：**One month**

一月[yī yuè]：**January**

一天[yì tiān]：**one day** 天[Tiān]：**day**

e.g. ● 他要在这里住一年。[Tā yào zài zhèlǐ zhù yì nián]

He will live here for one year.

● 一年有多少个月。[Yì nián yǒu duōshao ge yuè]

How many months are there in one year?

● 今天是10月1日/号。[Jīntiān shì shí yuè yī rì\hào]

Today is 1st October.

● 六月我很忙。[Liùyuè wǒ hěn máng]

I will be busy in June.

Quiz

I. Pronunciation.

  1. Please choose the initials or finals you heard.

    1) A. rì   B. rè

 2) A. kùn   B. hùn
 3) A. máo   B. móu
 4) A. shàng   B. sàng

2. Please choose the Pinyin you heard.

 1) A. liánxì   B. liángxí
 2) A. jīnnián   B. jīngyàn
 3) A. jīxīn   B. zhīxīn
 4) A. zájì   B. zázhì

II. Form sentences.

1. zhège   hěn   yuè   máng   wǒ
   1   2   3   4   5
   _____

2. shì   yuè   jīntiān   shíwǔ   hào   yī
   1   2   3   4   5   6
   _____

3. wǒ   zài   zhù   yào   liǎng   nián   Shànghǎi
   1   2   3   4   5   6   7
   _____

4. wǒ   jīpiào   hào   xiǎng   èrshíqī   de   mǎi
   1   2   3   4   5   6   7
   _____

III. Please translate the following sentences into Chinese.

1. This year is 2015.

   _____

2. I want to study Chinese on October, 6th.

   _____

3. How many days are there in a month?

   _____

4. How many months are there in a year?

   _____

This Week

Welcome to Elementary Level Three, Lesson Three of our **ChineseAny** podcast series teaching Chinese. Today we will learn three time-related words.

"*zuótiān 昨天*", yesterday.

> 昨天
> [zuótiān]
> yesterday   noun

"*qùnián 去年*", last year.
The year which has passed.

> 去年
> [qùnián]
> last year   noun

"*xīngqī 星期*", week.

> 星期
> [xīngqī]
> week   noun

So when referring to a DAY, we have learned "*jīntiān 今天*", today; "*míngtiān 明天*", tomorrow; "*zuótiān 昨天*", yesterday.

For the YEAR, we have learned "*jīnnián* 今年", this year; "*míngnián* 明年", next year; "*qùnián* 去年", last year. "*qù* 去" means "go", the year has gone.

OK, let's look at the last word, "*xīngqī* 星期". We put the number after it which makes "Monday, Tuesday ..., all the way to Saturday". But Sunday is a special one. We need to say "*xīngqī tiān* 星期天".

星期
[xīngqī]
week   noun

Please read the names of the days of the WEEK in Chinese.

星期一　[xīngqī yī]
Monday

星期二　[xīngqī èr]
Tuesday

星期三　[xīngqī sān]
Wednesday

星期四　[xīngqī sì]
Thursday

星期五　[xīngqī wǔ]
Friday

星期六　[xīngqī liù]
Saturday

星期天　[xīngqī tiān]
Sunday

Great, let's do some exercises to review what we have learned today.

● 昨天是星期五。

[Zuótiān shì xīngqī wǔ]

Yesterday was Friday.

● 这个星期三我们不工作。

[Zhège xīngqī sān wǒmen bù gōngzuò]

We don't work this Wednesday.

● 你们一个星期工作多少天?

[Nǐmen yí ge xīngqī gōngzuò duōshǎo tiān]

How many days do you work in one week?

● 这个星期我很忙。

[Zhège xīngqī wǒ hěn máng]

I'm very busy this week.

● 下个星期我不工作。

[Xià ge xīngqī wǒ bù gōngzuò]

Next week I don't work.

● 这个星期天你去书店吗?

[Zhège xīngqī tiān nǐ qù shūdiàn ma]

Are you going to the book store this Sunday?

Great, so that wraps up today's lesson. Hope you have learned something useful. You can download our app to access our Chinese lessons and learn Chinese anywhere, anytime with **ChineseAny**.

Word List

Main Vocabulary		
昨天 [zuótiān] yesterday	去年 [qùnián] last year	星期 [xīngqī] week
Additional Vocabulary		
星期一 [xīngqīyī] Monday	星期二 [xīngqī'èr] Tuesday	星期三 [xīngqīsān] Wednesday
星期四 [xīngqīsì] Thursday	星期五 [xīngqīwǔ] Friday	星期六 [xīngqīliù] Saturday
星期天 (日) [xīngqītiān (rì)] Sunday		

Notes

星期 [xīngqī] **week**：

星期 [xīngqī] **+ numerals (from 1 to 6)**：**weekdays**

星期天 [xīngqī tiān] \ 星期日 [xīngqīrì]：**Sunday**

Quiz

I. Pronunciation.

  1. Please choose the initials or finals you heard.

    1) A. xǐ   B. qǐ

    2) A. hān   B. hāng

3) A. yín   B. yíng

4) A. lè   B. nè

2. Please choose the Pinyin you heard.

1) A. bù jí   B. bùzhì

2) A. qiánxiàn   B. qiānxiàn

3) A. xīngqī   B. xīnqíng

4) A. jīntiān   B. jīngtiān

II. Form sentences.

1. <u>wǒmen</u>   <u>bù</u>   <u>xīngqīliù</u>   <u>gōngzuò</u>
     1   2   3   4

2. <u>zhège</u>   <u>wǒ</u>   <u>chī</u>   <u>xīngqī</u>   <u>zǎofàn</u>   <u>bù</u>
     1   2   3   4   5   6

3. <u>xiàge</u>   <u>ma</u>   <u>nǐ</u>   <u>yě</u>   <u>xīngqī</u>   <u>qù</u>
     1   2   3   4   5   6

4. <u>chī</u>   <u>wǒmen</u>   <u>qù</u>   <u>xīngqītiān</u>   <u>fàndiàn</u>   <u>fàn</u>
     1   2   3   4   5   6

III. Please translate the following sentences into Chinese.

1. Yesterday was Friday.

2. I do not work in next week.

3. I am very busy on Sunday.

4. See you next Tuesday.

What Time Is It Now

Welcome to Elementary Level Three, Lesson Four of our **ChineseAny** podcast series teaching Chinese. Today we will learn how to express the time of the day, three new words. Let's look at them now.

The 1st one, "*xiànzài* 现在", "now, at present, right now". we normally use it as a **TIME WORD**, which would be placed after the subject and before the verb.

> 现在
> [xiànzài]
> right now   noun

For example：

- 现在他很忙。[Xiànzài tā hěn máng]
  He is busy right now.

- 她现在不在。[Tā xiànzài bú zài]
  She is not in right now.

- 我们现在不知道。[Wǒmén xiànzài bù zhīdào]
  We don't know right now.

- 你现在在哪儿? [Nǐ xiànzài zài nǎr]
  Where are you now?

The 2nd one is "*diǎn* 点", o'clock. We put the number before it to express the time.

For example, one o'clock, you may say "*yī diǎn* 一点".

> 点
> [diǎn]
> o'clock   noun

However, please pay attention to the difference between "*yī diǎn* 一点" and a previous phrase we learned, "*yìdiǎnr* 一点儿", which means "a little bit". For "*yìdiǎnr* 一点儿" the "*yī* 一" is in the 4th tone and we need add the "*er*" at the end.

一点 [yī diǎn] one o'clock 一点儿 [yì diǎnr] a little bit

One thing we need to pay attention to is that "Two o'clock" in Chinese should be "*liǎng diǎn* 两点", not "*èr diǎn* 二点".

You may add the morning, afternoon, or evening before the time to distinguish between "A. M. " and "P. M. "

Two O'clock
两点　　~~二点~~ [liǎng diǎn]　[èr diǎn]

For example：

- 8 a. m. should be "*zǎoshàng bā diǎn* 早上八点".
  Eight o'clock in the morning.
- 8 p. m. should be "*wǎnshàng bā diǎn* 晚上八点".
  Eight o'clock in the evening.
- 3 p. m. should be "*xiàwǔ sān diǎn* 下午三点".
  Three o'clock in the afternoon.

OK, the last word is "*fēn* 分", minute.

Yes，it's the same character as "cent", but the meaning is different in this context. So let's try to do the following exercises.

分 [fēn] minute　noun

For example：

- 早上八点零五分. [zǎoshàng bā diǎn líng wǔ fēn.]
  8：05 a. m.

If the minute value is between 01 – 09, we need to add the "零
líng" before the minute.

- 上午九点十分。[shàngwǔ jiǔ diǎn shí fēn]
  9:10 a.m.

For the minute values up to TEN, we need to say "分 *fēn*".
But for the other minutes above ten, the "分 *fēn*" can be omitted.
For example:

- 上午十点二十。[shàngwǔ shí diǎn èrshí (fēn)]
  10:20 a.m.

- 下午两点四十。[xiàwǔ liǎng diǎn sìshí (fēn)]
  2:40 p.m.

Great, let's do some exercises to review what we learned today.

- 他今天下午2:20 去机场。
  [Tā jīntiān xiàwǔ liǎng diǎn èrshí qù jīchǎng]
  He will go to the airport at 2:20 p.m. today.

- 我们今天早上7点吃早饭。
  [Wǒmen jīntiān zǎoshàng 7diǎn chī zǎofàn]
  We'll have breakfast at
  7:00 a.m. today.

- 我想看下午3点的电影。
  [Wǒ xiǎng kàn xiàwǔ sāndiǎn de diànyǐng]
  I want to watch the movie at 3 p.m.

- 现在没有出租车。
  [Xiànzài méiyǒu chūzū chē]
  There is no taxi right now.

● 我不知道你九点来。

[Wǒ bù zhīdào nǐ jiǔ diǎn lái]

I didn't know you would come at 9:00.

● 我们明天6:40吃晚饭。

[Wǒmen míngtiān liùdiǎn sìshí chī wǎnfàn]

We'll have dinner at 6:40 p.m. tomorrow.

● 九点去有点儿晚。

[Jiǔdiǎn qù yǒudiǎnr wǎn]

It's a little late to go at 9:00.

● 我早上8点进了停车场。

[Wǒ zǎoshang bā diǎn jìn le tíngchē chǎng]

I entered the parking lot at 8 a.m.

Great, so that wraps up today's lesson. Hope you have learned something. Download our app to access our Chinese lessons. Remember, you can learn Chinese anywhere, anytime with **ChineseAny**.

Word List

Main Vocabulary		
现在[xiànzài] now	点[diǎn] o'clock	分[fēn] minute

Notes

① **点**[diǎn] **O'clock**：

- **Number + 点**[diǎn]：**to express the time**

  一点儿 [yìdiǎnr]：**a little bit**

  e.g. 1:00 一点[Yīdiǎn]　　2:00 两点[Liǎngdiǎn]

  　　 5:00 五点[Wǔdiǎn]　10:00 十点[Shídiǎn]

- **AM/PM**

  e.g. 8 a.m.　早上八点[Zǎoshang bā diǎn]

  　　 3 p.m.　下午三点[Xiàwǔ sān diǎn]

  　　 10 p.m.　下午十点[Xiàwǔ shí diǎn]

② **"分**[fēn]**" minute**：

the minute values up to ten + 分[fēn]

the minutes above ten, the 分[fēn]**can be omitted.**

e.g. 8:05 a.m.　早上 8:05 [Zǎoshang bā diǎn líng wǔ fēn]

　　 10:20 a.m.　上午 10:20 [Shàngwǔ shí diǎn èrshí (fēn)]

　　 2:40 p.m.　下午 2:40 [Xiàwǔ liǎng diǎn sìshí (fēn)]

Quiz

I. Pronunciation.

1. Please choose the initials or finals you heard.

   1) A. tì　　　　　　　B. dì

   2) A. qiā　　　　　　B. qiāo

   3) A. wèn　　　　　　B. wèng

   4) A. chù　　　　　　B. qù

2. Please choose the Pinyin you heard.

1) A. xiànzài   B. xiàn zhāi

2) A. sì fēn   B. shífēn

3) A. jǐ diǎn   B. jǐ jiàn

4) A. qī diǎn   B. qǐdiǎn

II. Form sentences.

1. shì   xiànzài   wǔ   shí   fēn   diǎn
   1   2   3   4   5   6

   _____

2. diǎn   wǒmen   shí   xuéxí   jīntiān
   1   2   3   4   5

   _____

3. wǒ   diǎn   zǎoshang   gōngzuò   bā
   1   2   3   4   5

   _____

4. wǒ   bú   xiānsheng   zài   jiā   xiànzài
   1   2   3   4   5   6

   _____

III. Please translate the following sentences into Chinese.

1. We do not have Chinese teacher now.

   _____

2. My family is not in China now.

   _____

3. I will go to see you at five o'clock.

   _____

4. It is ten past two now.

   _____

I'm on the 2nd Floor

Welcome to Elementary Level Three, Lesson Five of our **ChineseAny** podcast series teaching Mandarin Chinese. Today we will learn three characters. Let's look at them now.

The 1st one, "*bàn* 半", half.

We may use "O'clock +"*bàn* 半" to express the time.

For example：

- 五点半 [wǔ diǎn bàn]

  half past 5

- 我们七点半学习汉语。[Wǒmén qīdiǎn bàn xuéxí Hànyǔ]

  We will learn Chinese at 7:30 p.m.

> 半
> [bàn]
> half   number

We may also use it as a number；you need to add the measure word and noun after it.

For example,

- 半个中国人 [bàn gè Zhōngguó rén]

  Half Chinese

> 半 + counting word + noun
> [bàn]
> half of + noun

- 我是半个中国人,爸爸是美国人,妈妈是中国人。[Wǒ shì bàn ge Zhōngguó rén, bàba shì Měiguó rén, māma shì Zhōngguó rén]

  I'm half Chinese；my Dad is from USA, and Mom is from China.

- 我有半瓶水。[Wǒ yǒu bàn píng shuǐ]

  I have half bottle of water.

OK, the 2nd character is "*hào* 号".
We have learned this character twice
before.

> 号
> [hào]
> Building number   noun

- The first meaning is "number."
  We say "*hàomǎ* 号码", which
  means "room or phone number".
- The second meaning is "date."
  We say "*jīntiān shì wǔ hào* 今天是
  五号". Today is date 5th.

> 号
> [hào] { Number
>   Date
>   Building number

Today, we will express a building
number. So, let's see the 3rd character,
that is "*lóu* 楼".

> 楼 [lóu] { Building
>   Floor

"*lóu* 楼" has two meanings in Chinese. It can mean "building" and
can mean "floor." Please pay attention to the difference between them.
For example：

- Building No. 2 in Chinese is "*èr hào lóu* 二号楼".
- 2nd floor in Chinese is："*èr lóu* 二楼", there is no "*hào* 号".
- "My home is on the 3rd floor of Building No. 3" in Chinese would
  be："*Wǒ de jiā zài sān hào lóu , sān lóu* 我的家在3号楼,3楼"

Great, let's learn something else.
We have learned "*shàngwǔ* 上午" and "*xiàwǔ* 下午". We know
"*wǔ* 午" is noon, "*shàng* 上" means "up", "*xià* 下" means "down".
So "*lóuxià* 楼下" means "downstairs". "*lóushàng* 楼上"means
"upstairs". But "*shànglóu* 上楼" changes to a verb, which means "go

upstairs". "*xiàlóu* 下楼" means "go downstairs". But for today's lesson, all you need to remember is "*lóushàng* 楼上" and "*lóuxià* 楼下".

Great, let's do some exercises to review what we learned today.

● 我在二楼工作。
[Wǒ zài èrlóu gōngzuò]
I work on the 2nd floor.

● 我们住在三号楼。
[Wǒmen zhù zài sān hào lóu]
We live in Building No. 3.

● 我们去那个楼。
[Wǒmen qù nà gè lóu]
Let's go to that building.

● 前边的楼很好看。
[Qiánbiān de lóu hěn hǎokàn]
The building in front is nice.

● 书店在七楼。
[Shūdiàn zài qī lóu]
The book store is on the 7th floor.

● 我家楼下没有人。
[Wǒ jiā lóuxià méiyǒu rén]
There is nobody at my basement.

● 这里可以上楼。
[Zhèlǐ kěyǐ shàng lóu]
You can go upstairs here.

● 楼下停水了。
[Lóuxià tíng shuǐ le]
There is no water downstairs.

Great, so that wraps up today's lesson. Hope you have learned something. Download our app to access our Chinese lessons. Remember, you can learn Chinese anywhere, anytime with **ChineseAny**.

◯ Word List

Main Vocabulary		
半[bàn] half	号[hào] number, date	楼[lóu] floor, building
Additional Vocabulary		
楼上[lóushàng] upstairs	楼下[lóuxià] downstairs	上楼[shànglóu] go upstairs
下楼[xiàlóu] go downstairs		

◯ Notes

① 号[hào]**&** 楼[lóu]**:**

➤ 号[hào]**: 1. date 2. room or phone number 3. building number.**

e. g. ● 二号楼[èr hào lóu]

Building No. 2

● 我们住在三号楼。[Wǒmen zhù zài sān hào lóu]

We live in Building No. 3.

➤ "楼[lóu]": **1. building 2. floor**

e. g. ● 我们去那个楼。[Wǒmen qù nà ge lóu]

Let's go to that building.

● 书店在七楼。[Shūdiàn zài qī lóu]

The book store is on the 7th floor.

Quiz

I. Pronunciation.

1. Please choose the initials or finals you heard.

   1) A. bàn   B. pàn
   2) A. luó   B. lóu
   3) A. qià   B. xià
   4) A. niú   B. liú

2. Please choose the Pinyin you heard.

   1) A. yíbàn   B. yìbān
   2) A. bǎo le   B. pǎo le
   3) A. lòu xià   B. liúxià
   4) A. zhòngyào   B. zhōngyào

II. Form sentences.

1. diǎn   xiànzài   liǎng   bàn   shì
    1   2   3   4   5
   _____

2. bàn   tā   gè   Zhōngguó   shì   rén
    1   2   3   4   5   6
   _____

3. lóu   zhè   sān   ma   hào   shì
    1   2   3   4   5   6
   _____

4. wǒ   lóu   xuéxí   zài   wǔ   Hànyǔ
    1   2   3   4   5   6
   _____

III. Please translate the following sentences into Chinese.

    1. I still have half bottle of water.

    _____

    2. We live there.

    _____

    3. Do you live at 35th floor?

    _____

    4. Tomorrow Building No. 6 will be power cut.

    _____

What Time Is It Now

Welcome to Level Three, Lesson Six of our **ChineseAny** podcast series teaching Mandarin Chinese. Today we will learn three new words. One special question word and two nouns.

Let's look at two nouns first.

The 1st one, "*gōngsī 公司*" "company, office".

For example：

公司
[gōngsī]
company noun

● 这是我的公司。[Zhè shì wǒ de gōngsī]
This is my company.

● 我在公司。[Wǒ zài gōngsī]
I'm in the office.

● 我明天早上八点去公司。[Wǒ míngtiān zǎoshàng bā diǎn qù gōngsī]
I will go to the office at 8:00 a.m. tomorrow.

● 我在德国公司工作。[Wǒ zài Déguó gōngsī gōngzuò]
I work at a German company.

The 2nd character is "*huǒchē zhàn 火车站*", railway/train station.

"*huǒ 火*" means "fire"; "*chē 车*" means "car"; "*huǒchē 火车*" together means "train".

火车站
[huǒchē zhàn]
railway/train station noun

So "train ticket" is "*huǒchē piào* 火车票".

"*zhàn* 站" as a noun, means "station". You may say "*chēzhàn* 车站" for any kind of station, like bus station or subway station.

For example：

- 我去火车站买火车票。［Wǒ qù huǒchē zhàn mǎi huǒchē piào］
  I will go to the railway station to buy a ticket.

- 火车站有很多人。［Huǒchē zhàn yǒu hěn duō rén］
  There are too many people at the station.

- 上海有三个火车站。［Shànghǎi yǒu sān ge huǒchē zhàn］
  There are 3 railway stations in Shanghai.

OK, let's study the last new word, "*jǐ* 几".

"*jǐ* 几" has two useful meanings in Chinese.

The 1st meaning is "several".

You may add a counting word after it.

For example：

几
［jǐ］
several numbers

- 几个朋友［jǐ ge péngyǒu］
  several friends

- 几杯咖啡［jǐ bēi kāfēi］
  several cups of coffee

- 几瓶啤酒［jǐ píng píjiǔ］
  several bottles of beer

- 几本书［jǐ běn shū］
  several books

- 几天［jǐ tiān］
  several days

- 这几天［zhè jǐ tiān］
  these days

The 2nd meaning of "*jǐ* 几" is used as "a special question word" to ask "How many or how much". We use it to ask for a number.

> 几
> [jǐ]
> How many
> Special question word

You have previously learned "*duōshǎo* 多少" to ask "how many, how much".

Today, I will explain the difference between "*duōshǎo* 多少" and "*jǐ* 几".

The quantity implied by saying "*duōshǎo* 多少" is greater than that by "*jǐ* 几".

> 几 [jǐ]
> Less than 10
> 多少 [duōshǎo]
> more than 10

If we say "*jǐ* 几", it implies less than 10 of something. "*duōshǎo* 多少" would imply more than 10.

For example：

- 你有几个朋友? [Nǐ yǒu jǐ ge péngyǒu]
  How many friends do you have?
  The answer is expected to be around 2 – 10.

- 你有多少个朋友? [Nǐ yǒu duōshǎo ge péngyǒu]
  How many friends do you have?
  The answer is expected to be 10 or more.

- 你去北京几天? [Nǐ qù Běijīng jǐ tiān]
  How many days will you be in Beijing?
  The answer is expected to be 2 – 10 days.

- 你去北京多少天? [Nǐ qù Běijīng duōshǎo tiān]
  How many days will you be in Beijing?
  The answer is expected to more than 10, maybe for one month.

Another difference is that we must use a measure word after "*jǐ* 几".

But for "*duōshǎo* 多少", the measure word can be used or can be omitted.

Great, let's do some exercises to review what we learned today.

● 现在几点?
[Xiànzài jǐ diǎn]
What time is it right now?

● 明天星期几?
[Míngtiān xīngqī jǐ]
What day is tomorrow?

● 今天几号?
[Jīntiān jǐ hào]
What's the date today?

● 你家住在几楼?
[Nǐ jiā zhù zài jǐ lóu]
Which floor is your home?

● 你早上几点工作?
[Nǐ zǎoshàng jǐ diǎn gōngzuò]
What time do you start work in the morning?

● 今天几点吃晚饭?
[Jīntiān jǐ diǎn chī wǎnfàn]
What time shall we have dinner today?

● 你的朋友在哪个公司工作?
[Nǐde péngyǒu zài nǎge gōngsī gōngzuò]
Which company does your friend work for?

● 上海有多少咖啡店?
[Shànghǎi yǒu duōshǎo kāfēi diàn]
How many coffee shops are there in Shanghai?

Great, so that wraps up today's lesson. Hope you have learned something useful. Download our app to access our Chinese lessons. Remember, you can learn Chinese anywhere, anytime with **ChineseAny**.

Word List

Main Vocabulary		
公司[gōngsī] company, office	火车站[huǒchē zhàn] railway/train station	几[jǐ] how many, several
Additional Vocabulary		
火车[huǒchē] train	火车票[huǒchē piào] train ticket	站 [zhàn] station
车站[chēzhàn] bus/subway station		

Notes

① 几[jǐ] & 多少[duōshao]：**how many/how much**

  ➢ 多少[duōshao]：**more than 10 of something.**

  ➢ 几[jǐ]：**less than 10 of something.**

e. g. ● 你有几个朋友？[Nǐ yǒu jǐ ge péngyou]

     How many friends do you have?

     (The answer is expected to be around 2 – 10.)

    ● 你有多少个朋友？[Nǐ yǒu duōshao ge péngyou]

     How many friends do you have?

     (The answer is expected to be 10 or more.)

② 几[jǐ]：**two useful meanings.**

  ➢ **The 1st：several**

e.g. ● 我有几个中国朋友。［Wǒ yǒu jǐ ge Zhōngguó péngyǒu］
I have several Chinese friends.

● 我想买几杯咖啡。［Wǒ xiǎng mǎi jǐ bēi kāfēi］
I want to buy several cups of coffee.

➤ **The 2nd：used as a special question word to ask.**

e.g. ● 今天几号?［Jīntiān jǐ hào］
What's the date today?

● 明天星期几?［Míngtiān xīngqī jǐ］
What day will be tomorrow?

● 你早上几点工作?［Nǐ zǎoshang jǐ diǎn gōngzuò］
What time do you start your work in the morning?

Quiz

I. Pronunciation.

1. Please choose the initials or finals you heard.

    1) A. cē   B. chē

    2) A. huǒ   B. guǒ

    3) A. yuè   B. yùn

    4) A. lǎo   B. nǎo

2. Please choose the Pinyin you heard.

    1) A. gōngsī   B. gōngshì

    2) A. jǐ kē   B. jǐ gè

    3) A. chēzhàn   B. chēzhǎn

    4) A. huǒchē   B. huòchē

II. Form sentences.

1. <u>nǐ</u>　<u>jǐ</u>　<u>gōngsī</u>　<u>lóu</u>　<u>de</u>　<u>zài</u>
　　1　　2　　　3　　　4　　5　　6

_____

2. <u>gōngsī</u>　<u>xiànzài</u>　<u>nǐ</u>　<u>zài</u>　<u>nǎge</u>
　　　1　　　　2　　　3　　4　　5

_____

3. <u>jǐ</u>　<u>Shànghǎi</u>　<u>gè</u>　<u>huǒchēzhàn</u>　<u>yǒu</u>
　1　　　2　　　3　　　4　　　　5

_____

4. <u>hào</u>　<u>nǐ</u>　<u>qù</u>　<u>jǐ</u>　<u>Běijīng</u>
　　1　　2　　3　　4　　5

_____

III. Please translate the following sentences into Chinese.

1. What day is it tomorrow?

_____

2. How many days are there in a week?

_____

3. What is the date today?

_____

4. How many bottles of beer can you drink?

_____

How Many People Are There in Your Family

Welcome to Elementary Level Three, Lesson Seven of our **ChineseAny** podcast series teaching Mandarin Chinese. Today we will learn three new words: one measure word and two nouns. Let's look at them now.

The 1st character is " *kǒu* 口 ".

" *kǒu* 口 " has 3 basic meanings in Chinese. Today we will learn one of them, which is a measure word; we use it to express the number of family members.

口
[kǒu]
number of family members
measure word

Let's see the following two sentences:

- *Wǒ jiā yǒu sān kǒu rén.* 我家有三口人。
- *Wǒ jiā yǒu sān gè rén.* 我家有三个人。

" *gè* 个 " is the measure word, which is used for almost all nouns.

" *wǒ jiā yǒu sān gè rén.* 我家有三个人 ", there are 3 people in my home. They may be my friends, my guests, my students, or they can also be my family members. But " *wǒ jiā yǒu sān kǒu rén.* 我家有三口人 ", there are 3 family numbers in my family.

That's the difference between " *gè* 个 " and " *kǒu* 口 ". Hope that's clear.

OK, let's see the 2nd word, "*háizi 孩子*", child, kid.

The plural form can be "*háizi men 孩子们*". It includes sons and daughters and can also cover any kid.

For example：

- 他/她是我的孩子。[Tā shì wǒde háizi]
  He is my child (son)/she is my child (daughter).
- 他是一个好孩子。[Tā shì yí ge hǎo háizi]
  He is a good kid.

孩子
[háizi]
Child, kid　noun

The last word is "*érzi 儿子*", son.
For example：

- 我是爸爸,他是儿子。[Wǒshì bàba, tā shì érzi]
  I'm father, and he is son.
- 我姓王,我儿子也姓王。[Wǒ xìng Wáng, wǒ érzi yě xìng Wáng]
  My family name is Wang; my son also has the family name "Wang".

儿子
[érzi]
Son　Noun

OK, let's look at the family tree. Please repeat the names of family members.

爸爸 [bàba]
Father, Dad   noun

妈妈 [māma]
Mother, Mom   noun

儿子 [érzi]
Son   noun

女儿 [nǚér]
Daughter   noun

哥哥 [gēge]
Elder Brother   noun

弟弟 [dìdi]
Younger Brother   noun

姐姐 [jiějie]
Elder sister   noun

妹妹 [mèimei]
Younger sister   noun

You see, the second syllable of most family member names are in neutral tone.

Great, let's do some exercises to review what we have learned today.

● 你家有几口人?
[Nǐ jiā yǒu jǐ kǒu rén]
How many people are there in your family?

● 我家有三口人,爸爸,妈妈,我。
[Wǒ jiā yǒu sān kǒu rén, bàba, māma, wǒ]
My family has three people, my Dad, my Mom and I.

● 你有几个汉语老师?
  [Nǐ yǒu jǐ ge Hànyǔ lǎoshī]
  How many Chinese teachers do you have?

● 你可以喝几瓶啤酒?
  [Nǐ kěyǐ hē jǐ píng píjiǔ]
  How many bottles of beer can you drink?

● 你有多少中国朋友?
  [Nǐ yǒu duōshǎo Zhōngguó péngyou]
  How many Chinese friends do you have?

● 上海有几个机场?
  [Shànghǎi yǒu jǐ ge jīchǎng]
  How many airports are there in Shanghai?

● 你们公司有多少人?
  [Nǐmen gōngsī yǒu duōshǎo rén]
  How many people are there in your company?

● 我有一个儿子。
  [Wǒ yǒu yí ge érzi]
  I have one son.

Great, so that wraps up today's lesson. Hope you have learned something. Download our app to access our Chinese lessons and check out our next lesson to learn more Chinese with **ChineseAny**.

◯ Word List

Main Vocabulary		
口 [kǒu] a measure word for people in the family	孩子 [háizi] child, kid	儿子 [érzi] son

◯ Notes

口 [kǒu] & 个 [gè] :

口 [kǒu] : **the measure word, number of family members.**

个 [gè] : **the measure word.**

e. g. ● 我家有三口人，爸爸，妈妈，我。

　　　　[Wǒ jiā yǒu sān kǒu rén, bà ba, mā ma, wǒ]

　　　　My family has three people, my Dad, my Mom and I.

　　　● 我家有三个人。[Wǒ jiā yǒu sān ge rén]

　　　　There are 3 people in my home.

　　　● 你有几个汉语老师? [Nǐ yǒu jǐ ge Hànyǔ lǎoshī]

　　　　How many Chinese teachers do you have?

◯ Quiz

I. Pronunciation.

　1. Please choose the initials or finals you heard.

　　　1) A. ái　　　　　　　　B. ér

　　　2) A. jǐ　　　　　　　　B. qǐ

    3) A. xīn   B. qīn

    4) A. kǒu   B. hǒu

2. Please choose the Pinyin you heard.

    1) A. háizi   B. érzi

    2) A. chūkǒu   B. rùkǒu

    3) A. júzi   B. jùzi

    4) A. píjiǔ   B. píqiú

II. Form sentences.

1.
tā	sān	jiā	kǒu	yǒu	rén
1	2	3	4	5	6

2.
yǒu	liǎng	wǒmen	gè	háizi
1	2	3	4	5

3.
chūkǒu	tā	zài	hào	èr
1	2	3	4	5

4.
tā	jìnkǒu	xǐhuan	de	dōngxi	mǎi
1	2	3	4	5	6

III. Please translate the following sentences into Chinese.

1. How many people are there in your family?

2. How many Chinese teachers do you have?

3. How many bottles of water do you want to buy?

4. What time do you go to company on Monday?

I Love You

Welcome back to our **ChineseAny** podcast series where we teach Mandarin Chinese. This is Level Three, Lesson Eight. Today we will learn three new words: one particle and two verbs. Let's look at them now.

The 1st one is "*shàngbān 上班*". "Go to work". "*shàng 上*" is a verb here, which means "to go, to start". "*bān 班*" means "work, job".

上班
[shàngbān]
Go to work   Verb

Previously, we learned that "*shàng 上*" means morning or up and "*xià 下*" means afternoon or down.

So we may say "*xiàbān 下班*", which means "finish work, or leave work".

You may add a place before "*shàngbān 上班*", like "*Wǒ zài … gōngsī shàngbān 我在…公司上班*", which means "I work at … company".

Place + 上班
[shàngbān]
work at … place

Also you may add the time before "*shàngbān 上班*", like "*Wǒ jiǔdiǎn shàngbān 我九点上班*", which means "I go to work at nine o'clock".

Time + 上班
[shàngbān]
work at … time

For example：

- 你在哪儿上班? ［Nǐ zài nǎr shàngbān］
  Where do you work?

- 明天你几点上班? ［Míngtiān nǐ jǐ diǎn shàngbān］
  What time will you go to work tomorrow?

- 我这个星期四不上班。［Wǒ zhège xīngqī sì bú shàngbān］
  I don't work this Thursday.

- 我今天六点下班。［Wǒ jīntiān liùdiǎn xià bān］
  I will finish my work at six today.

As a verb, "*Shàng* 上" may also be used in "*shàng chē* 上车", which means "to get on the car" or "*shàng lóu* 上楼", which means "to go upstairs". For the antonyms, you may say "*xià chē* 下车" to express "get off the car" or "*xià lóu* 下楼", which means "to go downstairs".

These are the additional vocabularies for this lesson, please practice more.

The 2nd character is "*ài* 爱", to love.

> 爱
> ［ài］
> love   verb

You may use a noun after the "*ài* 爱". To say "I love my mom", "I love you", "I love China", you would say
"*wǒ ài wǒ de māma* 我爱我的妈妈",
"*wǒ ài nǐ* 我爱你", "*wǒ ài Zhōngguó* 我爱中国".

> Sb. + 爱 + Noun
> ［ài］
> Sb. love Sb/Sth.

Also you my use a verb phrase after it to express "love to do something".

> Sb. + 爱 + Verb
> [ài]
> Sb. love to do something.

If you put "*rén 人*" after "*ài 爱*", "*àirén 爱人*", it doesn't mean "lover". You can use this to refer to your husband or wife. It's very common in Chinese when introducing your husband or your wife to say "*Zhè shì wǒ àirén 这是我爱人*", "this is my husband or this is my wife".

Let's see some examples：
- 你爱我吗? [Nǐ ài wǒ ma]
  Do you love me?
- 我爱看电影。[Wǒ ài kàn diànyǐng]
  I love watching movie.
- 她爱学习汉语。[Tā ài xuéxí Hànyǔ]
  She loves learning Mandarin.
- 我们都爱吃水果。[Wǒmen dōu ài chī shuǐguǒ]
  We all love to eat fruit.

The last character is "*le 了*", neutral tone. It's a particle. In Chinese, "*le 了*" is one of the most difficult grammatical features in the Chinese language. English verbs are inflected for the present and past tense, like：eat-ate, sing-sang, work- worked. In Chinese,

> 了
> [le]
> Particle

normally we would just use "*le 了*" after the verb or at the end of a sentence to express the completion of some action or to express the past tense.

For example：

- 我晚上八点吃晚饭。[Wǒ wǎnshàng bā diǎn chī wǎnfàn]

  I eat dinner at 8：00 p. m.

  That is in the present tense.

- 我晚上八点吃晚饭了。[Wǒ wǎnshàng bā diǎn chī wǎnfàn le]

  I ate dinner at 8：00 p. m.

If the object after the verb is used with a measure word or has a specific quantity，it is preferable to put the "*le* 了" after the verb but before the object.

For example：

- 你买了几瓶水? [Nǐ mǎi le jǐ píng shuǐ]

  How many bottles of water did you buy?

- 我今天看了三场电影。[Wǒ jīntiān kàn le sān chǎng diànyǐng]

  I watched three movies today.

Great，let's do some exercises to review what we learned today.

- 你爱喝什么茶?

  [Nǐ ài hē shénme chá]

  What tea do you love to drink?

- 我爱我的家人。

  [Wǒ ài wǒ de jiārén]

  I love my families.

- 我早上八点半上班。

  [Wǒ zǎoshàng bā diǎn bàn shàngbān]

  I go to work at 8：30 a. m.

- 你在哪里上班?

  [Nǐ zài nǎlǐ shàngbān]

  Where do you work?

- 我喜欢坐出租车上班。
  [Wǒ xǐhuān zuò chūzū chē shàngbān]
  I like to go to work by taxi.

- 我爱人是美国人。
  [Wǒ àiren shì Měiguó rén]
  My wife is from USA.

Great, so that wraps up today's lesson. Hope you have learned something. Download our app to access our Chinese lessons and learn Chinese anywhere, anytime with **ChineseAny**.

Word List

Main Vocabulary		
上班[shàngbān] go to work	爱[ài] to love	了[le] particle
Additional Vocabulary		
下班[xiàbān] after\finish work, leave work for the day	爱人[àirén] husband or wife	上车[shàngchē] get on the car
下车[xiàchē] get off the car	上楼[shànglóu] go to the upstairs	下楼[xiàlóu] go to the downstairs

Notes

① 了[le] : **Subject + verb + noun + 了[le] or**

Subject + verb + 了[le] + noun

(to show the completion of some action or past tense).

e.g. ● 昨天他们去买东西了。[Zuótiān tāmen qù mǎi dōngxi le]

They went shopping yesterday.

● 今天我喝了一杯咖啡。[Jīntiān wǒ hē le yì bēi kāfēi]

I drank one cup of coffee today.

Quiz

I. Pronunciation.

1. Please choose the initials or finals you heard.

1) A. le   B. ne

2) A. sàng   B. shàng

3) A. xī   B. sī

4) A. zì   B. cì

2. Please choose the Pinyin you heard.

1) A. àirén   B. ǎirén

2) A. nǚhái   B. nǚ'ér

3) A. shànglóu   B. sānlóu

4) A. zuò chē   B. zū chē

II. Form sentences.

1. <u>wǒ</u>   <u>gōngzuò</u>   <u>de</u>   <u>háizi</u>   <u>le</u>
   1   2   3   4   5

2. <u>chī</u>   <u>nǐ</u>   <u>ma</u>   <u>zǎofàn</u>   <u>le</u>
   1   2   3   4   5

3. <u>zuótiān</u>   <u>liǎng</u>   <u>wǒ</u>   <u>le</u>   <u>píng</u>   <u>hē</u>   <u>píjiǔ</u>
    1   2   3   4   5   6   7

4. <u>sān</u>   <u>tā</u>   <u>le</u>   <u>běn</u>   <u>mǎi</u>   <u>shū</u>
   1   2   3   4   5   6

III. Please translate the following sentences into Chinese.

1. What time do you go to work?

2. What do you love to drink?

3. He cooked a lot of dishes.

4. She called two taxis.

Who Are You Looking for

Welcome to Elementary Level Three, Lesson Nine of our **ChineseAny** podcast series teaching Mandarin Chinese. Today we will learn three characters: one measure word, one verb, and one special question word. Let's look at them now.

The 1st vocabulary, "*wèi* 位". It's a polite measure word for people.

Up until now, we have learned three ways of counting people.

位
[wèi]
measure word for people

Can you remember all of them? They are "*gè* 个", "*kǒu* 口", and "*wèi* 位". Could you please tell me the difference among them?

个	口	位
[gè]	[kǒu]	[wèi]

- "*gè* 个" is just to express the number of people, and it can be used to refer to the number of objects.
- "*kǒu* 口" is only used for the number of family members.
- "*wèi* 位" is used to express the number of people in a polite way such as towards a client, guest, or customer.

For example,

➢ When you enter a restaurant, the waiter would ask you "how many of you, sir?"

In Chinese, this would be

"*Qǐng wèn , xiānshēng , nín jǐ wèi* 请问,先生,您几位?"

Your answer would be "*sān wèi , xièxie* 三位,谢谢!", Table for 3, thank you!

➤ Also, when you introduce somebody,

If you say "*Zhè gè (rén) shì wǒ de lǎoshī* 这个人是我的老师", there is no grammatical mistake. But it's similar to saying "this person is my teacher" in English, It's a bit impolite.

But if we say "*Zhè wèi shì wǒ de lǎoshī* 这位是我的老师", that could be "this lady/gentleman is my teacher"

The 2nd character is "*zhǎo* 找", to "look for".

找
[zhǎo]
to look for   verb

For example：

- 你找什么? [Nǐ zhǎo shénme]
  What are you looking for?
- 我找我的手机。[Wǒ zhǎo wǒ de shǒujī]
  I'm looking for my cell phone.
- 难找[nán zhǎo]
  It's hard/difficult to find
- 很难找[sth hěn nán zhǎo]
  sth. is hard to find

OK, let's look at the 3rd character, "*shuí* 谁",

This is a special question word which means "who or whom". In Chinese

谁
[shuí]
who/whom
Special question word

sentence structure，it can be used as subject or as the Object.

For example：

- 你是谁？［Nǐ shì shuí］

  Who are you?

- 你找谁？［Nǐ zhǎo shuí］

  Who are you looking for?

- 谁是你的汉语老师？［Shuí shì nǐ de hànyǔ lǎoshī］

- 你的汉语老师是谁？［Nǐ de hànyǔ lǎoshī shì shuí］

  Who is your Chinese teacher?

  These above two sentences share the same meaning.

We have learned "*nǐde* 你的"，means "yours" and "*wǒde* 我的" means mine. So "whose" in Chinese is "*shuí de* 谁的".

Let's see some examples：

- 这是谁的书？［Zhè shì shuí de shū］

  Whose book is this?

- 她是谁的太太？［Tā shì shuí de tàitai］

  Whose wife is she?

Great，let's do some exercises to review what we learned today.

- 请问，谁可以帮我？

  ［Qǐng wèn, shuí kěyǐ bāng wǒ］

  Excuse me, who can help me?

- 谁想喝咖啡？

  ［Shuí xiǎng hē kāfēi］

  Who would like to drink coffee?

- 哪位是索菲老师？

  ［Nǎ wèi shì Suǒfēi lǎoshī］

  Which one is Teacher. Sophie?

- 你是谁的老师？

  ［Nǐ shì shuí de lǎoshī］

  Whose teacher are you?

- 这些东西是谁的？
  [Zhèxiē dōngxi shì shuí de]
  Whose things are these?

- 谁不喜欢吃米饭？
  [Shuí bù xǐhuān chī mǐfàn]
  Who doesn't like rice?

Great, so that wraps up today's lesson. Hope you have learned something useful. Download our app to access our Chinese lessons. Remember, you can learn Chinese anywhere, anytime with **ChineseAny**.

Word List

Main Vocabulary		
位[wèi] a polite counting word for people	谁[shuí] who，whom	找[zhǎo] to look for
Additional Vocabulary		
谁的[shuíde] whose		

Notes

① 谁[shuí]：**who/whom**；谁的[shuíde]：**whose**：
    e.g. ● 谁是你的汉语老师？[Shuí shì nǐ de Hànyǔ lǎoshī]
           Who is your Chinese teacher?

- 这是谁的书？［Zhè shì shuí de shū］
  Whose book is this?

- 她是谁的太太？［Tā shì shuí de tàitai］
  Whose wife is she?

② 个［gè］，口［kǒu］，位［wèi］

个［gè］：**number of people or objects.**

口［kǒu］：**number of family members.**

位［wèi］：**polite measure word for people.**

e. g. ● 这个东西是谁的？［Zhège dōngxi shì shuí de］
  Whose thing is this?

- 我家有三口人。［Wǒ jiā yǒu sān kǒu rén］
  There are three people in my family.

- 这位是我的老师。［Zhè wèi shì wǒ de lǎoshī］
  This lady/gentleman is my teacher.

Quiz

I. Pronunciation.

1. Please choose the initials or finals you heard.

　　1) A. huī　　　　　　　　B. hēi

　　2) A. zǎo　　　　　　　　B. zhǎo

　　3) A. zuǒ　　　　　　　　B. zǒu

　　4) A. shéi　　　　　　　　B. shén

2. Please choose the Pinyin you heard.

　　1) A. zhào shàng　　　　B. zǎoshang

　　2) A. shéide　　　　　　　B. shuíde

　　3) A. kǒuzi　　　　　　　B. kòuzi

　　4) A. zhīdào　　　　　　　B. chídào

II. Form sentences.

1. <u>wǒ</u>   <u>tā</u>   <u>bù</u>   <u>zhǎo</u>   <u>zhīdào</u>   <u>shéi</u>
    1   2   3   4   5   6

_____

2. <u>jǐ</u>   <u>nǐmen</u>   <u>xiānsheng</u>   <u>wèi</u>
  1   2   3   4

_____

3. <u>nǐ</u>   <u>shéi</u>   <u>qǐngwèn</u>   <u>zhǎo</u>
  1   2   3   4

_____

4. <u>zhè</u>   <u>shéide</u>   <u>bēi</u>   <u>shì</u>   <u>kāfēi</u>
  1   2   3   4   5

_____

III. Please translate the following sentences into Chinese.

1. Who is your Chinese teacher?

_____

2. What are you looking for?

_____

3. She wants to look for a Chinese teacher.

_____

4. Who can help me?

_____

Female and Male

Welcome to Elementary Level Three, Lesson Ten of our **ChineseAny** podcast series teaching Mandarin Chinese. Today we will learn three adjectives. Let's look at them now.

The first two adjectives are "*nǚ* 女" and "*nán* 男", female and male. You may add a noun after them.

For example：

女	
[nǚ]	
female	adjective

- "*nǚ* 女" + "*péngyǒu* 朋友", girlfriend.

"*nǚ* 女" + "*xǐshǒu jiān* 洗手间", female washroom.

"*nǚ* 女" + "*lǎoshī* 老师", female teacher.

"*nǚ* 女" + "*háizi* 孩子", female kid, girl.

"*nǚ* 女" + "*rén* 人", woman.

"*nǚ* 女" + "*de* 的", which means "female", you may have a noun after it.

The same can be done for male，

"*nán* 男" + "*péngyǒu* 朋友", boyfriend.

"*nán* 男" + "*xǐshǒu jiān* 洗手间", male washroom.

男	
[nán]	
Male	adjective

"*nán* 男" + "*lǎoshī* 老师", male teacher.

"*nán* 男" + "*háizi* 孩子", male kid, boy.

"*nán* 男" + "*rén* 人", man.

"*nán* 男" + "*de* 的", which means "male, you may have a noun after it".

One thing we need to pay attention to is that "*nán péngyǒu* 男朋友*"* means "boyfriend" but "*nán de péngyǒu* 男的朋友*"* means "male friend".

For example：

"*Tā shì wǒ de nán péngyǒu* 他是我的男朋友*"* and "*Tā shì wǒ nán de péngyǒu* 他是我男的朋友*"* are totally different, so please be careful！The same for "*nǚ péngyǒu* 女朋友*"*. "*nǚ péngyǒu* 女朋友*"* means "girlfriend" but "*nǚ de péngyǒu* 女的朋友*"* means "female friend". The last thing we need to pay attention to is that "*nǚ* 女*"* and "*nán* 男*"* can only be used for people, not for animals.

Let's see some examples：

● 请问，女洗手间在哪儿？［Qǐng wèn, nǚ xǐshǒu jiān zài nǎr］
   Excuse me, where is the female washroom?
● 那个男老师不在这儿工作。［Nà ge nán lǎoshī bú zài zhèr gōngzuò］
   That male teacher doesn't work here.
● 我女朋友去书店了。［Wǒ nǚ péngyou qù shūdiàn le］
   My girlfriend went to the book store.
● 那个女人是有钱人。［Nàge nǚrén shì yǒuqián rén］
   That woman is rich.

OK, the 3rd adjective is "*piàoliàng* 漂亮*"*, beautiful. We usually use it to describe a female；

漂亮
［piàoliàng］
beautiful   adjective

sometimes we also use it for a beautiful sight or view.

You may say "*hěn piàoliàng* 很漂亮*"*, very beautiful；"*bú piàoliàng* 不漂亮*"*, not beautiful.

For example：

- 这个孩子很漂亮。[Zhè ge háizi hěn piàoliàng]
  This kid is very pretty.

- 你们公司谁漂亮？[Nǐmen gōngsī shuí piàoliàng]
  Who is beautiful in your company?

- 她的孩子们都不漂亮。[Tā de háizi men dōu bú piàoliàng]
  Her kids are all not beautiful.

- 那个漂亮的女人是谁？[Nà ge piàoliàng de nǚrén shì shuí]
  Who is that beautiful lady?

Great，let's do some exercises to review what we learned today.

- 我帮她找男朋友。
  [Wǒ bāng tā zhǎo nán péngyou]
  I will help her to find a boyfriend.

- 这位是我的女朋友。
  [Zhè wèi shì wǒde nǚ péngyou]
  This is my girlfriend.

- 我的老师是女的。
  [Wǒ de lǎoshī shì nǚde]
  My teacher is a female.

- 他的朋友都是男的。
  [Tā de péngyou dōu shì nánde]
  All of his friends are male.

- 他的女朋友很漂亮。
  [Tā de nǚ péngyou hěn piàoliàng]
  His girlfriend is beautiful.

- 我们都喜欢女老师。
  [Wǒmen dōu xǐhuān nǚ lǎoshī]
  We all like female teachers.

- 他没有女朋友。
  [Tā méiyǒu nǚ péngyou]
  He doesn't have girlfriend.

- 我想请一位男老师。
  [Wǒ xiǎng qǐng yí wèi nán lǎoshī]
  I want a male teacher.

● 女人都喜欢买东西。
[Nǚrén dōu xǐhuān mǎi dōngxi]
All women like going shopping.

● 你喜欢男孩子还是女孩子？
[Nǐ xǐhuān nán háizi háishì nǚ háizi]
Would you like a girl or boy?

Great，so that wraps up today's lesson. Hope you have learned something. Download our app to access our Chinese lessons and learn Chinese anywhere，anytime with **ChineseAny**.

Word List

Main Vocabulary		
女 [nǚ] female	男 [nán] male	漂亮 [piàoliang] pretty, beautiful
Additional Vocabulary		
男朋友 [nán péngyou] boy-friend	女朋友 [nǚ péngyou] girl-friend	女孩子 [nǚ háizi] girl = female kid
男孩子 [nán háizi] boy = male kid	男人 [nán rén] man	女人 [nǚrén] woman
男的 [nán de] male	女的 [nǚ de] female	

Notes

的 [de]：**adj + 的 [de] + noun**

e. g. ● 他是我的好朋友。[Tā shì wǒde hǎo péngyou]

He is my good friend.

● 我们是很好的朋友。[Wǒmen shì hěn hǎo de péngyou]

We are the best friends.

● 他有一个漂亮的女朋友。[Tā yǒu yí gè piàoliang de nǚ péngyou]

He has a pretty girlfriend.

Quiz

I. Pronunciation.

1. Please choose the initials or finals you heard.

1) A. sè　　　　　　　　B. shè

2) A. qiū　　　　　　　　B. jiū

3) A. lù　　　　　　　　B. nù

4) A. piào　　　　　　　B. biào

2. Please choose the Pinyin you heard.

1) A. piàoliang　　　　　B. biāoliàng

2) A. nǚrén　　　　　　B. lùrén

3) A. nánrén　　　　　　B. lǎn rén

4) A. nánnǚ　　　　　　B. lán lù

II. Form sentences.

1. <u>nǐ</u>　　<u>shì</u>　　<u>lǎoshī</u>　　<u>nánde</u>　　<u>nǚde</u>　　<u>háishi</u>
　　1　　2　　　3　　　　4　　　　5　　　　6

2. <u>shéi</u>　　<u>péngyou</u>　　<u>tā</u>　　<u>shì</u>　　<u>nǚ</u>
　　1　　　　2　　　　3　　4　　5

3. shéi   háizi   de   piàoliang   nàge   shì
   1   2   3   4   5   6

_____

4. dōngxi   xīhuan   nǚrén   mǎi
   1   2   3   4

_____

III. Please translate the following sentences into Chinese.

1. Who do you think is pretty?

_____

2. Do you like female teacher or male teacher?

_____

3. I think she looks a little nicer.

_____

4. She likes to buy delicious things.

_____

Hello，Everyone

Welcome back to our *ChineseAny* podcast series where we teach Mandarin Chinese. This is Level Three, Lesson Eleven. Today we will learn three new words：one interjection, one verb, and one pronoun.

The 1st one is "*wèi* 喂", "*wèi* 喂" is often glossed as an **INTERJECTION** for an informal greeting, an expression equivalent to "hello" or "hey" in English.

> 喂
> [wèi]
> informal greeting
> Interjection

It is, however, used most often as **a telephone greeting**, similar to using "hello" when answering a phone call. When speaking to a person face-to-face, however, it is very impolite to "greet" the others by saying "*wèi* 喂". To address someone with "*wèi* 喂" is like saying to them "Hey, you!" in English. Only when speaking to a very close friend or wanting the attention of a total stranger would one use "*wèi* 喂" as a "greeting" interjection. But it sounds rude.

When we use "*wèi* 喂" to answer a phone call, it is always pronounced in the 2nd tone verbally.

For example：

- 喂,你好！请问,你找谁？［Wèi, nǐ hǎo! Qǐng wèn, nǐ zhǎo shuí］
  Hello！Whom do you want to speak to?

- 喂,是北京饭店吗？［Wèi, shì Běijīng fàndiàn ma］
  Hello！Is that Beijing Hotel?

The 2nd character is "*rènshí* 认识", to know.

Before we learned "*zhīdào* 知道", which also means "to know".

认识
[rènshí]
to know   verb

Today let's learn the difference between them. "*zhīdào* 知道" is to know of something or someone even if you do not have direct experience with it.

For example：

- 我知道中国。[Wǒ zhīdào Zhōngguó]
  I know China.
  (You may know of China，but maybe you've never been there.)
- 我知道迈克尔乔丹。[Wǒ zhīdào Màikèěr · qiáodān]
  I know Michael Jordan.
  (You may know of Michael Jordan，but maybe you've never met him.)

"*rènshí* 认识" is to know somebody or something after you've met or interacted with them/it.

For example：

- 我认识汉字。[Wǒ rènshi hànzì]
  I know Chinese characters (I can recognize Chinese characters).
  (If you look at Chinese characters and you understand them.)
- 我认识迈克尔乔丹。[Wǒ rènshi Màikèěr · qiáodān]
  I know Michael Jordan.
  (It means you have met him or you are his friend.)

If you want to say you "recognize" someone or something，even if you've never met or interacted with them/it，you **CAN** say "*rènshí* 认识" as well as "*zhīdào* 知道". In this case，to say "I recognize Michael Jordan"，even if you haven't met him，you can also say "*Wǒ rènshi/*

zhīdào Michael Jordan 我认识/知道迈克尔乔丹" or "*Wǒ bú rènshi hànzì* 我不认识汉字", I don't know Chinese characters.

OK，let's look at the following dialogue to review these two verbs.

A：你知道姚明吗？［Nǐ zhīdào Yáomíng ma］

　　Do you know Yaoming?

B：我知道，他是中国人。［Wǒ zhīdào，tā shì Zhōngguó rén］

　　I know. He is Chinese.

A：你认识姚明吗？［Nǐ rènshi Yáomíng ma］

　　Do you know Yaoming?

B：不认识。［Bú rènshi］

　　I don't know.

The 3rd word is "*dàjiā* 大家"，"*dàjiā* 大家" means "everybody"，it is a **noun**. "*dà* 大" means "big, large, huge". "*jiā* 家" means "family". A big family must have many people, so we use "*dàjiā* 大家" to greet many people present.

> 大家
> ［dàjiā］
> everybody　noun

We learned "*rén* 人"，person, people, so "*jiārén* 家人" means "family".

For example：

● 大家都喜欢这个老师。［Dàjiā dōu xǐhuan zhè ge lǎoshī］

　　Everyone likes this teacher.

● 大家都认识他。［Dàjiā dōu rènshi tā］

　　Everybody knows him.

● 很高兴认识大家。［Hěn gāoxìng rènshi dàjiā］

　　Nice to meet everybody.

Great, let's learn something more. We learned "*bēi* 杯", the cup; "*píng* 瓶", the bottle; "*hào* 号", number. All these words can be used as **NOUNS** and can also as measure **WORDS**.

大 + Noun
[dà]
big

So "large cup" in Chinese is "*dàbēi* 大杯". "big bottle" in Chinese is "*dàpíng* 大瓶", and "*dàhào* 大号" means "big size".

For example：

- 我要大杯的卡布其诺。[Wǒ yào dàbēi de kǎ bù qí nuò]
  I want a large cup of cappuccino.

- 请给我一大瓶水。[Qǐng gěi wǒ yí dà píng shuǐ]
  Please give me a big bottle of water.

- 我想买大号的。[Wǒ xiǎng mǎi dà hào de]
  I want to buy the large size one.

Great, let's do some exercises to review what we've learned today.

- 喂！是三星公司吗？
  [Wèi! Shì Sānxīng gōngsī ma]
  Hello！Is that Samsung Company？

- 今天大家都很忙。
  [Jīntiān dàjiā dōu hěn máng]
  Everyone is busy today.

- 大家都喜欢这个音乐。
  [Dàjiā dōu xǐhuan zhè ge yīnyuè]
  Everyone likes this music.

- 我认识他的太太。
  [Wǒ rènshi tā de tàitai]
  I know his wife.

- 我知道这个名字，我不认识他。
  [Wǒ zhīdào zhè ge míngzi, wǒ bú rènshi tā]
  I know this name, but I don't know him.

- 大家好，很高兴认识你们。
  [Dàjiā hǎo, hěn gāoxìng rènshi nǐmen]
  Hello, everybody, glad to meet you！

Great, so that wraps up today's lesson. Hope you have learned something. You can download our app to access our collection of Chinese lessons. Remember, you can learn Chinese anywhere, anytime with **ChineseAny**.

Word List

Main Vocabulary		
喂[wèi] hello	认识[rènshi] to know	大家[dàjiā] everyone
Additional Vocabulary		
大[dà] big	家[jiā] home	大杯[dàbēi] big cup of
家人[jiārén] family	大瓶[dàpíng] big bottle of	大号[dàhào] big size

Notes

① **认识** [rènshi] **to know, to recognize**
   认识[rènshi] **+ person or road**
   e.g. ● 我认识他的汉语老师。[Wǒ rènshi tā de Hànyǔ lǎoshī]
      I know his Chinese teacher.
      ● 没关系，师傅，我认识路。[Méi guānxi, shīfu, wǒ rènshi lù]
      It does not matter, Sir. I know the road.

② **知道** [zhīdào] **& 认识** [rènshi]：
   知道[zhīdào] **+ everything/everyone**
   认识[rènshi] **+ (only) person/road**

e. g. ● 我知道索菲。

［Wǒ zhīdào Suǒfēi］I know Sophie.

（You only know the name）

● 我认识索菲。

［Wǒ rènshi Suǒfēi］I recognize Sophie.（personally）

● 我认识他的家人。

［Wǒ rènshi tā de jiārén］

I know his family.（personally）

● 我知道她是谁。

［Wǒ zhīdào tā shì shuí］I know who she is.

（You know who she is, but may not know her）

Quiz

I. Pronunciation.

1. Please choose the initials or finals you heard.

1）A. luò   B. lòu

2）A. sān   B. shān

3）A. wán   B. wáng

4）A. hǎi   B. gǎi

2. Please choose the Pinyin you heard.

1）A. rènshi   B. rènzhī

2）A. dàjiā   B. dǎjiǎ

3）A. huí jiā   B. guī jiā

4）A. tóngzhì   B. tōngzhī

II. Form sentences.

1. <u>dàjiā</u>   <u>kāfēi</u>   <u>dōu</u>   <u>hē</u>   <u>xǐhuan</u>
      1   2   3   4   5

    _____

2. <u>nǐ</u>   <u>ma</u>   <u>tā</u>   <u>rènshi</u>   <u>bù</u>
     1   2   3   4   5

    _____

3. <u>gāoxìng</u>   <u>nǐ</u>   <u>hěn</u>   <u>rènshi</u>
       1   2   3   4

    _____

4. <u>rènshi</u>   <u>nǚ</u>   <u>wǒ</u>   <u>bù</u>   <u>péngyou</u>   <u>tā</u>
      1   2   3   4   5   6

    _____

III. Please translate the following sentences into Chinese.

1. Do you know her Chinese teacher?

    _____

2. Hello everyone, I am Sophie, your Chinese friend.

    _____

3. Everybody likes to watch that movie.

    _____

4. Who do you know?

    _____

Make a Phone Call

Welcome to Elementary Level Three, Lesson Twelve of our **ChineseAny** podcast series teaching Chinese. Today we will learn four words: two verbs, one noun, and one colloguial word.

The 1st one is "*diànhuà* 电话", "*diànhuà* 电话" means "telephone". "*diàn* 电" means "electricity", "*huà* 话" means "words", the words from the electronic machine, which in Chinese is "*diànhuà* 电话". Before we learned "*hàomǎ* 号码", number, so telephone number is "*diànhuà hàomǎ* 电话号码".

电话
[diànhuà]
telephone   noun

For example:

- 你知道他的电话号码吗? [Nǐ zhīdào tā de diànhuà hàomǎ ma]
  Do you know his telephone number?
- 他的电话号码是什么? [Tā de diànhuà hàomǎ shì shénme]
  What is his telephone number?
  It is also correct to say:
  "*Tā de diànhuà hàomǎ shì duōshao* 他的电话号码是多少? "

The 2nd word is "*dǎ* 打". "*dǎ* 打" is a **VERB**, which has many meanings in Chinese, like "to play, to beat, to call". In today's lesson, we will use the meaning

打
[dǎ]
to dial/make (a call)
verb

"to dial", "to make (a call) , so "to make a phone call" in Chinese is "*dǎ diànhuà* 打电话", you also may say "*dǎ yí ge diànhuà* 打一个电话", to make **a** phone call.

The 3rd character is "*gěi* 给". "*gěi* 给" has two important meanings in Chinese. The 1st one is used as a **VERB**, which means "to give".

给	
[gěi]	
to give	verb
for	preposition

Normally we may use the phrase "**S + gěi +Sb. + Sth.**"
We may use dual objects after it.

S + gěi +Sb. + Sth.
（O1） （O2）

For example：

- 他给了我一本英语书。[Tā gěi le wǒ yì běn Yīngyǔ shū]
  He gave me one English book.
- 我昨天给了他很多电影票。[Wǒ zuótiān gěi le tā hěn duō diànyǐng piào]
  I gave him many movie tickets yesterday.
- 妈妈给了孩子一百元。[Māma gěi le háizi yì bǎi yuán]
  Mother gave the child one hundred yuan.

The 2nd meaning is as a **PREPOSITION**, which means "do sth. **for** sb. / do sth. **to** sb. "

But in Chinese, we should say "gěi **给 + sb. + do sth.** "
For example：

Gěi 给 + sb. + do sth.
do sth. for sb/
do sth. to sb.

- 给你打电话。[gěi nǐ dǎ diànhuà]
  Make a phone call **to** you.

- 给你买咖啡。[gěi nǐ mǎi kāfēi]
  Buy coffee **for** you.
- 我给家人做早饭。[Wǒ gěi jiārén zuò zǎofàn]
  I make breakfast **for** my family.

OK，after these three words，let's learn one more thing.

We learned "*huà* 话" in this lesson，it means "words". We learned "*shuō* 说" previously，which means "to say，to speak"，so "to talk or to say something"，in Chinese is "*shuōhuà* 说话".

For example：

- 他不喜欢说话。[Tā bù xǐhuan shuōhuà]
  He doesn't like to talk.
- 你说话很好听！[Nǐ shuōhuà hěn hǎotīng]
  You speak so nicely！
- 请不要说话！[Qǐng búyào shuōhuà]
  Please don't talk！

Great，let's do some exercises to review what we learned today.

- 可以给我一杯咖啡吗？
  [Kěyǐ gěi wǒ yì bēi kāfēi ma]
  May I have a cup of coffee？

- 他昨天给我打了一个电话。
  [Zuótiān tā gěi wǒ dǎ le yí ge diànhuà]
  He called me yesterday.

● 今天有我的电话吗?
[Jīntiān yǒu wǒ de diànhuà ma]
Did somebody call me today?

● 我想给他买一本书。
[Wǒ xiǎng gěi tā mǎi yì běn shū]
I want to buy one book for him.

Great, so that wraps up today's lesson. Hope you have learned something useful. Download our app to access our Chinese lessons. As always, you can learn Chinese anywhere, anytime with **ChineseAny**.

Word List

Main Vocabulary		
电话[diànhuà] telephone	打[dǎ] to dial	给[gěi] to give, for/to
Additional Vocabulary		
话[huà] word	说话[shuōhuà] to speak/say	

Notes

① 给[gěi]
  ➤ Sb. + 给[gěi] + Sb. + Sth.

e.g. ● 请给我你的电话号码。[Qǐng gěi wǒ nǐ de diànhuà hàomǎ]
Please give me your phone number.

● 他给了我一杯咖啡。[Tā gěi le wǒ yì bēi kāfēi]
He gave me a cup of coffee.

➤ 给[gěi] + sb. + do sth (do sth. for sb./do sth. to sb.)

e.g. ● 他们给我买了很多汉语书。
[Tāmen gěi wǒ mǎi le hěn duō Hànyǔ shū]
They bought lots of Chinese books for me.

● 明天早上我给你打电话。
[Míngtiān zǎoshang wǒ gěi nǐ dǎ diànhuà]
I will call you tomorrow morning.

Quiz

I. Pronunciation.

1. Please choose the initials or finals you heard.

　　1) A. lǎng　　　　　　　B. lǎn

　　2) A. chī　　　　　　　 B. cī

　　3) A. yá　　　　　　　　B. yé

　　4) A. nǔ　　　　　　　　B. nǚ

2. Please choose the Pinyin you heard.

　　1) A. diànhuà　　　　　 B. duǎn huà

　　2) A. dǎ chē　　　　　　B. dā chē

　　3) A. dàrén　　　　　　 B. dǎrén

　　4) A. piányi　　　　　　 B. biǎnyì

II. Form sentences.

1. <u>wǒ</u>   <u>zhè</u>   <u>diànhuà</u>   <u>shì</u>   <u>de</u>
      1   2   3   4   5

    _____

2. <u>kāfēi</u>   <u>kěyǐ</u>   <u>bēi</u>   <u>gěi</u>   <u>wǒ</u>   <u>yì</u>   <u>ma</u>
      1   2   3   4   5   6   7

    _____

3. <u>gěi</u>   <u>tā</u>   <u>shénme</u>   <u>mǎi</u>   <u>le</u>   <u>nǐ</u>
      1   2   3   4   5   6

    _____

4. <u>jīntiān</u>   <u>ma</u>   <u>wǒde</u>   <u>yǒu</u>   <u>diànhuà</u>
       1   2   3   4   5

    _____

III. Please translate the following sentences into Chinese.

1. Can you call me tomorrow morning?

    _____

2. I bought a mobile phone to her.

    _____

3. Please give me a cup of tea.

    _____

4. What did you give her?

    _____

You and Me

Welcome to Elementary Level Three, Lesson Thirteen of our **ChineseAny** podcast series teaching Mandarin Chinese. Today we will learn three words: one noun, one conjunction, and one particle.

The 1st character is "*diànnǎo 电脑*", computer. "*diàn 电*" means "electricity", "*nǎo 脑*" means "brain".

电脑
[diànnǎo]
computer   noun

Previously we learned "*diànyǐng 电影*", "*diànhuà 电话*". So "*diàn 电*" can be followed by a **NOUN**, it means "the thing related to the electricity".

For example:

- 这是谁的电脑? [Zhè shì shuí de diànnǎo]
  Whose computer is this?

- 你的电脑多少钱? [Nǐ de diànnǎo duōshao qián]
  How much is your computer?

- 他的电脑很好看。[Tā de diànnǎo hěn hǎokàn]
  His computer looks nice.

- 我没有电脑。[Wǒ méiyǒu diànnǎo]
  I have no computer.

The 2nd word is "*hé 和*". "*hé 和*" "and" in English.

We use it to connect **NOUNS**,

和
[hé]
and   conjunction

PRONOUNS, and **NOMINAL EXPRESSIONS**.

You may say "*nǐ hé wǒ 你和我*", "you and me".

When the subject phrase contains two or more nouns joined together by "*hé 和*", the predicate is usually preceded by **the adverb** "*dōu 都*" which indicates plurality of the subject.

OK, let's look at some sentences：

● 我学习英语和法语。[Wǒ xuéxí Yīngyǔ hé Fǎyǔ]
I am studying English and French.

● 爸爸、妈妈和弟弟都在家。[Bàba, māma hé dìdi dōu zài jiā]
Father, mother and little brother are all at home.

There is one point we need to pay attention to is "*hé 和*". Unlike "and" in English, "*hé 和*" is never used to connect clauses. It also is never used to connect verbs or adjectives.

For example：

● 我买火车票,和他买飞机票。
[Wǒ mǎi huǒchē piào, hé tā mǎi fēijī piào] (✗)
我买火车票,他买飞机票。
[Wǒ mǎi huǒchē piào, tā mǎi fēijī piào] (√)
I will buy a train ticket, and he will buy a plane ticket.

● 我很累,和她也很累。[Wǒ hěn lèi, hé tā yě hěn lèi] (✗)
我很累,她也很累。[Wǒ hěn lèi, tā yě hěn lèi] (√)
I'm tired, and she is also tired.

The 3rd character is "*ba 吧*".

Firstly, "*ba 吧*" is a **PARTICLE** which is attached to the end of a sentence to **signal a request or a suggestion**.

For example：

● 我们喝一杯咖啡吧。[Wǒmen hē yì bēi kāfēi ba]

吧
[ba]　particle

Let's have a cup of coffee.

- 我们去公司吧。［Wǒmen qù gōngsī ba］
  Let's go to the office.

- 你来这儿吧。［Nǐ lái zhèr ba］
  How about you coming here?

- 我给你做饭吧。［Wǒ gěi nǐ zuòfàn ba］
  Let me cook for you.

Secondly，"ba 吧" is used to indicate **uncertainty or supposition**. When added to a statement，it is used to imply that the speaker is merely making a suggestion or an estimation with abatement of tone.

For example：

- 你是中国人吧？［Nǐ shì Zhōngguó rén ba］
  You are Chinese, right?

- 今天是星期一吧？［Jīntiān shì xīngqī yī ba］
  Today is Monday, right?

- 这里是浦东机场吧？［Zhèlǐ shì Pǔdōng jīchǎng ba］
  Here is Pudong airport, right?

- 您是王老师吧？［Nín shì Wáng lǎoshī ba］
  You are Mr. Wang（teacher），right?

Great，let's compare the differences between the two particles，"ma 吗" and "ba 吧" when they're used in questions. We use "ma 吗" for "**YES or NO question**".

For example：

- 你是中国人吗？［Nǐ shì Zhōngguó rén ma］
  Are you Chinese?

- 你是中国人吧？［Nǐ shì Zhōngguó rén ba］
  You are Chinese, right?

Great, let's do some exercises to review what we learned today.

● 我们明天去看电影吧。

[Wǒmen míngtiān qù kàn diànyǐng ba]

Let's go to watch a movie tomorrow.

● 我们今天晚上吃泰国菜吧。

[Wǒmen jīntiān wǎnshang chī Tàiguó cài ba]

Let's go to have Thai food tonight.

● 你和我都是美国人。

[Nǐ hé wǒ dōu shì Měiguó rén]

You and I are all from USA.

● 今天晚上我和朋友去喝啤酒。

[Jīntiān wǎnshang wǒ hé péngyou qù hē píjiǔ]

I'll go to drink beer with friends tonight.

Great, so that wraps up today's lesson. Hope you have learned something useful. Download our app to access our Chinese lessons. Remember, you can learn Chinese anywhere, anytime with *ChineseAny*.

◖ **Word List**

Main Vocabulary		
电脑[diànnǎo] computer	和[hé] and/with	吧[ba] Let's/confirm question

Additional Vocabulary		
脑[nǎo] brain		

Notes

① **和**[hé]：**and/with**

   ➤ **Subject +和**[hé] **+ nouns/pronouns/nominal expressions**

e. g.　● 今天我和朋友去看电影。

      [Jīntiān wǒ hé péngyou qù kàn diànyǐng]

      Today I go to watch a movie with friend.

     ● 我可以说汉语和英语。

      [Wǒ kěyǐ shuō Hànyǔ hé Yīngyǔ]

      I can speak Chinese and English.

   ➤ **和**[hé]**Noun/pronouns/nominal + 都**[dōu] **+ verb/adjective**

e. g.　● 我和他都喜欢吃意大利饭。

      [Wǒ hé tā dōu xǐhuan chī Yìdàlì fàn]

      He and I both like Italy food.

     ● 他和他的朋友都不知道。

      [Tā hé tā de péngyou dōu bù zhīdào]

      He and his friend don't know.

② **The particle 吧**[ba]

   ➤ **Sentence + 吧**[ba]：to **signal a request or a suggestion.**

e. g.　● 明天我们去买东西吧。[Míngtiān wǒmen qù mǎi dōngxi ba]

      Let's go shopping tomorrow.

     ● 你坐出租车去那儿吧。[Nǐ zuò chūzū chē qù nàr ba]

      You go there by taxi.

> Sentence + 吧[ba]：to indicate **uncertainty or supposition.**

e.g. ● 今天是一月十号吧？［Jīntiān shì yī yuè shí hào ba］
Today is January 10th，right？

    ● 那个女孩子是日本人吧？［Nà ge nǚ háizi shì Rìběn rén ba］
That girl is Japanese，right？

Quiz

I. Pronunciation.

  1. Please choose the initials or finals you heard.

    1）A. nǎo   B. rǎo

    2）A. bō   B. pō

    3）A. dié   B. děi

    4）A. kè   B. gè

  2. Please choose the Pinyin you heard.

    1）A. diànnǎo   B. tiānláo

    2）A. yí biàn   B. yí piàn

    3）A. nǎozi   B. lǎozi

    4）A. jiǔbā   B. jiǔ bǎ

II. Form sentences.

  1. zhè   diànhuà   shì   de   hàomǎ   wǒ
     1   2   3   4   5   6

  2. wǒmen   ba   kàn   xiàwǔ   diànyǐng   de
      1   2   3   4   5   6

  3. wǒ   hé   fàn   péngyou   fàndiàn   chī   qù
     1   2   3   4   5   6   7

4. xǐhuan   Hànyǔ   wǒ   péngyou   hé   yìqǐ   xué

    1   2   3   4   5   6   7

_____

III. Please translate the following sentences into Chinese.

1. Today I bought yogurt and bread.

_____

2. This is her mobile phone number, right?

_____

3. Let's go to buy things tomorrow.

_____

4. This is his computer.

_____

Let's Go

Welcome to Elementary Level Three, Lesson Fourteen of our **ChineseAny** podcast series teaching Mandarin Chinese. Today we will learn three words: one negative word and two verbs.

The 1st character is "*méi* 没", "*méi* 没" is a **NEGATIVE WORD**, like "*bù* 不".

> 没
> [méi]
> didn't   negation word

We use "*bù* 不" in the **present and future tense**, We can use a **VERB or ADJECTIVE** after it.

> 不 + Verb/Adj. +
> [bù] { Present tense
>   Future tense

But "*méi* 没" is for **past tense**, and we can only use a **VERB** after it.

> 没 + verb + Present tense
> [méi]

For example:
- 我今天没吃早饭。[Wǒ jīntiān méi chī zǎofàn]
  I didn't have breakfast this morning.
- 我昨天没买水果。[Wǒ zuótiān méi mǎi shuǐguǒ]
  I didn't buy fruits yesterday.
- 现在我不去机场。[Xiànzài wǒ bú qù jīchǎng]

Now I don't go to the airport.

- 我星期六不忙。[Wǒ xīngqī liù bù máng]
  I'm not busy on Saturday.

The 2nd character is "*gàosù* 告诉", to tell. It is a **VERB**. You may use **two objects** after it, "*gàosù* 告诉" + **Sb.** + **Sth.**

告诉
[gàosù]
tell   verb

Please pay attention to the difference between "*shuō* 说" **and** "*gàosù* 告诉".

We need put the content of what is being said，not Sb.，after "*shuō* 说". But we must put Sb. after "*gàosù* 告诉".

告诉 + Sb. + Sth.
[gàosù]
tell sb. sth.

For example：

- 请告诉我他的电话号码。[Qǐng gàosù wǒ tā de diànhuà hàomǎ]
  Please tell me his phone number.

- 他没告诉我他的名字。[Tā méi gàosù wǒ tā de míngzì]
  He didn't tell me his name.

- 请不要告诉他。[Qǐng bú yào gàosù tā]
  Please don't tell him.

- 你告诉了他什么？[Nǐ gàosù le tā shénme]
  What did you tell him?

The 3rd character, "*zǒu* 走". "*zǒu* 走" means "to go, to walk, to move".

Previously we learned "*qù* 去" means "to go", now let's see the difference between "*qù* 去" and "*zǒu* 走".

走
[zǒu]
to walk/to leave   verb

➤ "*qù* 去", means "to go to some place", so we must add a **location** after it.

> 去 + Location
> [qù]
> to go + location

➤ "*zǒu* 走" just means "to go, to leave", so we put **nothing** after it.

> 走 + nothing
> [zǒu]
> to go/to walk

For example：

● 我们去他的家。[Wǒmen qù tā de jiā]

We are going to his home.

● 我们去公司。[Wǒmen qù gōngsī]

We will go to the office.

● 我们去商店。[Wǒmen qù shāngdiàn]

We will go to the shop.

● 我们走吧。[Wǒmen zǒu ba]

Let's go！

● 他走了。[Tā zǒu le]

He left！

Great，let's do some exercises to review what we learned today.

● 她没有男朋友。
[Tā méiyǒu nán péngyou]
She has no boyfriend.

● 我走了，明天见。
[Wǒ zǒu le, míngtiān jiàn]
I'm leaving, and see you tomorrow.

● 他没告诉我。
[Tā méi gàosù wǒ]
He didn't tell me.

● 明天我们去北京。
[Míngtiān wǒmen qù Běijīng]
We will go to Beijing tomorrow.

Great, so that wraps up today's lesson. Hope you have learned something. Download our app to access our Chinese lessons. Remember, you can learn Chinese anywhere, anytime with *ChineseAny*.

Word List

Main Vocabulary		
没[méi] did not	告诉[gàosù] to tell	走[zǒu] to go/leave

Notes

① **没**[méi] **& 不**[bù]

➤ **没**[méi] **+ Verb**：this pattern is used in the past tense.

➤ **不**[bù] **+ Verb/adjective**：this pattern is used in the present and future tense.

e.g. ● 昨天我没去看电影。[Zuótiān wǒ méi qù kàn diànyǐng]
I did not go to watch a movie yesterday.

● 他没告诉我他住在那里。[Tā méi gàosù wǒ tā zhù zài nàlǐ]
He did not tell me he lived there.

● 妈妈不喜欢喝咖啡。[Māma bù xǐhuan hē kāfēi]
Mom doesn't like coffee.

● 今天我不工作。[Jīntiān wǒ bù gōngzuò]
I don't work today.

Quiz

I. Pronunciation.

1. Please choose the initials or finals you heard.

1) A. měi   B. mǒu

2) A. gào   B. kào

3) A. zuǒ   B. zǒu

4) A. shì   B. shù

2. Please choose the Pinyin you heard.

1) A. zuòtú   B. zǒulù

2) A. gàosù   B. gāochù

3) A. méishì   B. měishí

4) A. fèi   B. bèi

II. Form sentences.

1. <u>tā</u>   <u>hěn</u>   <u>gàosù</u>   <u>wǒ</u>   <u>nán</u>   <u>Hànyǔ</u>
    1   2   3   4   5   6

2. <u>zǎofàn</u>   <u>jīntiān</u>   <u>méi</u>   <u>chī</u>   <u>wǒ</u>
     1   2   3   4   5

3. <u>méi</u>   <u>nǐ</u>   <u>zǒu</u>   <u>wǎnshang</u>   <u>ma</u>
    1   2   3   4   5

4. <u>wǒ</u>   <u>bù</u>   <u>le</u>   <u>tā</u>   <u>qù</u>   <u>zhīdào</u>   <u>nǎr</u>
    1   2   3   4   5   6   7

III. Please translate the following sentences into Chinese.

1. Yesterday, she did not call me.

_____

2. Please tell me what your name is.

_____

3. That food is very nice, let's go to eat.

_____

4. I am leaving, see you tomorrow.

_____

I Have Known It Already

Welcome to Lesson Fifteen of our **ChineseAny** podcast series teaching Mandarin Chinese. Today we will learn three words：two adverbs and one conjunction. Let's look at them now.

The 1st character is "*dànshì* 但是". "*dànshì* 但是", is a conjunction, we use that to combine clauses.

> 但是
> [dànshì]
> but   conjunction

For example,

- 他是中国人,但是他不可以说汉语。[Tā shì Zhōngguó rén, dànshì tā bú kěyǐ shuō Hànyǔ]
  He is a Chinese, but cannot speak Chinese.

- 今天是星期一,但是我不工作。
  [Jīntiān shì xīngqī yī, dànshì wǒ bù gōngzuò]
  Today is Monday, but I'm not working.

The 2nd character is "*yǐjīng . . . le* 已经……了", "already", usually we put a verb between them. It means "to have done sth. already".

> 已经……了
> [yǐjīng . . . le]   already

For example,

- 他已经知道了。[Tā yǐjīng zhīdào le]
  He has known this already.

- 我已经给她打电话了。[Wǒ yǐjīng gěi tā dǎ diànhuà le]

I have called him already.

- 我已经说对不起了。［Wǒ yǐjīng shuō duìbuqǐ le］
  I have said "Sorry" already.

OK, let's move on to the 3rd character, "*hái* 还". "*hái* 还" is an adverb, It has three useful meanings in Chinese. Let's look at them now.

> 还
>
> ［hái］
>
> Still/else/not yet　adverb

➤ The 1st meaning is "else".

We usually use it before the verb to "express to do something else or to do something more".

For example,

- 我还想喝一杯茶。［Wǒ hái xiǎng hē yì bēi chá］
  I would like to drink one more cup of tea.
- 我有弟弟，还有妹妹。［Wǒ yǒu dìdi, háiyǒu mèimei］
  I have a younger brother；I also have younger sister.

➤ The 2nd meaning of "*hái* 还" is "still". We also need to use it before the verb.

For example,

- 我还在公司。［Wǒ hái zài gōngsī］
  I'm still in the office.
- 我们今天还吃米饭。［Wǒmen jīntiān hái chī mǐfàn］
  We are（still）eating rice again today.

➤ The 3rd meaning of "*hái* 还", is "not yet". We usually use it together with "*méi* 没", "*háiméi* 还没" and we must use it before a verb.

For example,

- 妈妈还没做饭。［Māma háiméi zuòfàn］
  Mom hasn't cook yet.

● 你还没给我啤酒。[Nǐ háiméi gěi wǒ píjiǔ]
You haven't given me the beer.

One thing we need to pay attention to, "*hái bù* 还不" means "still not". "*háiméi* 还没" means "not yet".

Great, let's do some exercises to review what we learned today.

● 谢谢, 我已经知道了。
[Xièxiè, wǒ yǐjīng zhīdào le]
Thank you, I have knew that already.

● 他还不知道我是谁。
[Tā hái bù zhīdào wǒ shì shéi]
He still doesn't know who I am.

● 这个很好吃, 但是太贵了。
[Zhè ge hěn hǎochī, dànshì tài guì le]
This is delicious, but it's too expensive.

● 我知道他的名字, 但是我不认识他。
[Wǒ zhīdào tā de míngzi, dànshì wǒ bú rènshi tā]
I know his name, but I don't know him.

Great, so that wraps up today's lesson. Hope you have learned something. Download our app to access our Chinese lessons and learn Chinese anywhere, anytime with **ChineseAny**.

Word List

Main Vocabulary		
但是 [dànshì] but	已经 [yǐjīng] already	还 [hái] still
Additional Vocabulary		
还没 [háiméi] not yet		

Notes

还 [hái] **It has three useful meanings：**

➢ **The 1st meaning is "else". 还** [hái] **+ noun \ verb**

e. g. ● 我家有牛奶,还有酸奶。[Wǒ jiā yǒu niúnǎi hái yǒu suānnǎi]

   We have milk，and yoghourt else in my home.

   ● 他可以说英语,还可以说汉语。[Tā kěyǐ shuō Yīngyǔ hái kěyǐ shuō Hànyǔ]

   He can speak English, and can speak Chinese else.

➢ **The 2nd meaning is "still". 还** [hái] **+ verb**

e. g. ● 这个星期六我们还去北京。[Zhège xīngqī liù wǒmen hái qù Běijīng]

   We still go to Beijing on this Saturday.

   ● 我们明天还吃这个吧。[Wǒmen míngtiān hái chī zhège ba]

   Let's still eat this tomorrow.

> **The 3rd meaning is 还没**[háiméi]：**not yet.**
> **还不**[hái bù]：**still not.**

e. g. ● 他们还没学习汉语。[Tāmen hái méi xuéxí Hànyǔ]

　　　They have not studied Chinese yet.

　　● 我还不知道他住在哪里。[Wǒ hái bù zhīdiào tā zhù zài nǎlǐ]

　　　I still do not know where he lives.

Quiz

I. Pronunciation.

　1. Please choose the initials or finals you heard.

　　1) A. sū　　　　　　　B. shū

　　2) A. lèi　　　　　　　B. liè

　　3) A. mén　　　　　　B. méng

　　4) A. nǐ　　　　　　　B. lǐ

　2. Please choose the Pinyin you heard.

　　1) A. dànshì　　　　　B. dāngshí

　　2) A. yǐjīng　　　　　B. yídìng

　　3) A. hái méi　　　　　B. hǎimián

　　4) A. dāngrán　　　　B. dànrán

II. Form sentences.

　1. $\underset{1}{\text{le}}$　$\underset{2}{\text{wǒ}}$　$\underset{3}{\text{chī}}$　$\underset{4}{\text{yī jīng}}$　$\underset{5}{\text{zǎofàn}}$

_____

　2. $\underset{1}{\text{wǒ}}$　$\underset{2}{\text{zài}}$　$\underset{3}{\text{xiànzài}}$　$\underset{4}{\text{hái}}$　$\underset{5}{\text{jiārén}}$　$\underset{6}{\text{Shànghǎi}}$

_____

3. <u>wǒ</u>　　<u>méi</u>　　<u>zuò</u>　　<u>hái</u>　　<u>wǎnfàn</u>
　　1　　　2　　　3　　　4　　　5

4. <u>tā</u>　<u>gěi</u>　<u>wǒ</u>　<u>yǐjīng</u>　<u>dǎ</u>　<u>le</u>　<u>diànhuà</u>
　　1　　2　　3　　　4　　　5　　6　　　7

III. Please translate the following sentences into Chinese.

1. That is very nice, but it is very expensive.

2. She wants to study Chinese, but she thinks it is very difficult.

3. I still have two weeks.

4. I have already bought that book.

Slow and Fast

Welcome to Elementary Level Three, Lesson Sixteen of our **ChineseAny** podcast series teaching Mandarin Chinese. Today we will learn three characters: two adjectives and one measure word. Let's have a look.

The 1st character is "*biàn* 遍", "*biàn* 遍" is a measure word. It means "time(s)".

遍
[biàn]
time　counting word

Usually we use that after the verb to express how many times an action happened.

Normally the verbs before it would be "to say", "to listen", "to write", "to see" and "to read".

VERB + Number + 遍
[biàn]

For example,

- 你可以再说一遍吗? [Nǐ kěyǐ zài shuō yí biàn ma]
  Can you say it one more time, please?
- 那个电影,我已经看了三遍了。[Nà ge diànyǐng wǒ yǐjīng kàn le sān biàn le]
  I have watched that movie three times.
- 我想再听一遍他的音乐。[Wǒ xiǎng zài tīng yí biàn tā de yīnyuè]
  I want to listen to his music one more time.

The 2nd vocabulary is an adjective "*kuài* 快", "*kuài* 快" means "fast".

快

[Kuài]

fast   adjective

You may say

- 很快 [hěn kuài]

  very fast

- 太快了 [tài kuài le]

  too fast

For example：

- 太快了,我来上海已经三年了。[Tài kuài le, wǒ lái Shànghǎi yǐjīng sān nián le]

  It is too fast, I have already been Shanghai for three years.

- 坐地铁去上班很快。[Zuò dìtiě qù shàngbān hěn kuài]

  It is fast to go to work by metro.

- 我想快一点儿去机场。[Wǒ xiǎng kuài yìdiǎnr qù jīchǎng]

  I want to go to the airport, faster.

The 3rd vocabulary is an adjective "*màn* 慢", "*màn* 慢" means "slow".

慢

[màn]

slow   adjective

You may say

- 慢一点儿 [màn yìdiǎnr]

  slow down

- 有点儿慢 [yǒudiǎnr màn]

  a little slow

For example：

- 请慢一点儿走。[Qǐng màn yìdiǎnr zǒu]

  Walk slowly.

- 我女朋友吃饭有点儿慢。[Wǒ nǚ péngyou chīfàn yǒudiǎnr màn]

  My girlfriend eats a little slowly.

- 你太慢了,可以快一点儿吗? [Nǐ tài màn le, kěyǐ kuài yìdiǎnr ma]

You are too slow, could you be faster?

- 我的汉语老师说话很慢。[Wǒ de Hànyǔ lǎoshī shuōhuà hěn màn]
  My Chinese teacher speaks very slowly.

Please pay attention here.

We use "*yǒudiǎnr 有点儿*" before the adjective when you don't feel very satisfied.

But we use "*yìdiǎnr 一点儿*" after the adjective to express the adjective in the comparative degree.

For example：

- 这个有点儿贵，你可以便宜一点儿吗？[Zhè ge yǒudiǎnr guì, nǐ kěyǐ piányì yìdiǎnr ma]
  This is a little expensive, can you make it cheaper?
- 我的朋友太少了，我想要多一点儿。[Wǒ de péngyǒu tài shǎo le, wǒ xiǎng yào duō yìdiǎnr]
  I have too few friends, I want more.

Great, let's look at some examples to practice what we learned today.

- 请再说一遍。
  [Qǐng zài shuō yí biàn]
  Please say it again.

- 我们可以再听一遍。
  [Wǒmen kěyǐ zài tīng yí biàn]
  We may listen to it one more time.

● 太快了，可以说慢一点儿吗？

[Tài kuài le, kěyǐ shuō màn yìdiǎnr ma]

It's too fast, can you say it slower?

● 我已经告诉你五遍了。

[Wǒ yǐjīng gàosù nǐ wǔ biàn le]

I have told you five times already.

Great, so that wraps up today's lesson. Hope you have learned something. Download our app to access all of our lessons and learn more Chinese with **ChineseAny**.

◗ **Word List**

Main Vocabulary		
遍[biàn] time（measure word）	快[kuài] fast	慢[màn] slow

◗ **Notes**

① 遍[biàn]　**time（measure word）**

Verb + Number +遍 biàn

e.g. ● 你说的电影我看了三遍。

[Nǐ shōu de diànyǐng wǒ kàn le sān biàn]

That movie you said has been watched three times.

- 我已经说了两遍了。[Wǒ yǐjīng shuō le liǎng biàn le]
  I have already said twice.
- 我们都问了一遍。[Wǒmen dōu wèn le yí biàn le]
  We all asked once.

② **有点儿**[yǒudiǎnr] **& 一点儿**[yìdiǎnr]

有点儿[yǒudiǎnr] **+ adjective**：not very satisfied.

Adjective + [yìdiǎnr]**一点儿**：you prefer.

e. g. ● 今天我有点儿累。[Jīntiān wǒ yǒu diǎnr lèi]
  I am a little tired today.
- 我们早上有点儿忙。[Wǒmen zǎoshang yǒudiǎnr máng]
  We are a little busy in the morning.
- 我的汉语不好，你可以说慢一点吗？
  [Wǒ de Hànyǔ bù hǎo, nǐ kěyǐ shuō màn yì diǎnr ma]
  My Chinese is not very good, could you speak a little slower?
- 我们快一点儿吧。[Wǒmen kuài yìdiǎnr ba]
  Let's go a little faster.

Quiz

I. Pronunciation.

1. Please choose the initials or finals you heard.

   1) A. xià   B. jià

   2) A. yě   B. liě

   3) A. lá   B. ná

   4) A. hài   B. huài

2. Please choose the Pinyin you heard.

   1) A. yí biàn   B. yìbiān

   2) A. héshuǐ   B. hē shuǐ

3) A. kuàimàn   B. guài màn

4) A. huìyì   B. huíyì

II. Form sentences.

1. <u>nǐ</u>   <u>màn</u>   <u>yìdiǎn</u>   <u>shuō</u>   <u>ma</u>   <u>kěyǐ</u>
   1   2   3   4   5   6

_____

2. <u>qǐng</u>   <u>shuō</u>   <u>yī</u>   <u>zài</u>   <u>biàn</u>
   1   2   3   4   5

_____

3. <u>kěyǐ</u>   <u>wǒmen</u>   <u>yí</u>   <u>tīng</u>   <u>zài</u>   <u>biàn</u>
   1   2   3   4   5   6

_____

4. <u>sān</u>   <u>yǐjīng</u>   <u>wǒmen</u>   <u>xué</u>   <u>le</u>   <u>biàn</u>
   1   2   3   4   5   6

_____

III. Please translate the following sentences into Chinese.

1. Could you speak one more time?

_____

2. My Chinese is not very good, please speak a little slower.

_____

3. Today has been already Friday.

_____

4. I want to read that book again.

_____

How Can I Do It

Welcome to Elementary Level Three, Lesson Seventeen of our **ChineseAny** podcast series teaching Mandarin Chinese. Today we will learn three words: one special question word and two nouns. Let's look at them now.

The 1st vocabulary is "*zěnme* 怎么", "*zěnme* 怎么" is a special question word. There are two meanings.

怎么
[zěnme]
how to
special question word

➢ The 1st meaning is "how to do". We use it before the **VERB**. An object can be placed after the verb.

（S.）+ 怎么 + Verb(+ O.)
[zěnme]
how to do

For example:

● 这个汉语怎么说? [Zhè ge Hànyǔ zěnme shuō]
How do you say this in Chinese?

● 你想怎么去北京? [Nǐ xiǎng zěnme qù Běijīng]
How would you like to go to Beijing?

● 你怎么知道他不喜欢? [Nǐ zěnme zhīdào tā bù xǐhuan]
How do you know that he doesn't like it?

● 你知道怎么去地铁站吗？［Nǐ zhīdao zěnme qù dìtiě zhàn ma］
Do you know how to go to the metro station?

➢　The 2nd meaning is "why".
We use it before a sentence, verb or adjective.

（S. ）＋怎么＋Verb（＋O.)/S/Adj.
　　　　［zěnme］

why

For example：
● 你怎么不给我打电话？［Nǐ zěnme bù gěi wǒ dǎ diànhuà］
Why don't you call me?

● 你怎么来晚了？［Nǐ zěnme lái wǎn le］
Why did you come late?

● 今天是星期一,你怎么不去上班？
［Jīntiān shì xīngqī yī,nǐ zěnme bú qù shàngbān］
Today is Monday, why don't you go to work?

● 你朋友怎么胖了？［Nǐ péngyou zěnme pàng le］
Why does your friend gain weight?

OK, the 2nd character is "lù
路", "lù　路" has two meanings,

路
［lù］
road　the number of bus

The 1st meaning is "road",
used as a noun. You may put the name of the road before it.
　e. g. ● 南京路［Nánjīng Lù］
　　　　　Nanjing Road.

　　　　● 龙阳路［Lóngyáng lù］
　　　　　Longyang Road.

- 我们公司在四川路上。[Wǒmen gōngsī zài Sìchuān lù shàng]
  My company is on Sichuan Road.
- 南京路上有很多饭店。[Nánjīng lù shàng yǒu hěn duō fàndiàn]
  There are a lot of restaurants on Nanjing road.

➤ The 2nd meaning is "a bus number".
  For example,
- 我坐211路车去机场。[Wǒ zuò 211 lù chē qù jīchǎng]
  I will go to the airport by No. 211 bus.
- 我们坐几路车去? [Wǒmen zuò jǐ lù chē qù]
  Which bus shall we take?
- 这儿没有五路车。[Zhèr méiyǒu wǔ lù chē]
  There is no NO. 5 bus here.

Today's 3rd word is "*shīfu* 师傅".
"*shīfu* 师傅" is a way to address
someone. Normally we use it to address a
skillful middle-aged men, like repairmen,
cleaners, drivers and so on.

师傅
[shīfu]
sir (driver)   noun

  For example：
- 师傅,你好,我去北京路。[Shīfu, nǐhǎo, wǒ qù Běijīng lù]
  Hello, Sir, I will go to Beijing road.
- 师傅,请给我发票。[Shīfu, qǐng gěi wǒ fāpiào]
  Sir, please give me the invoice.
- 师傅,你知道去陆家嘴怎么走吗? [Shīfu, nǐ zhīdào qù Lùjiāzuǐ zěnme zǒu ma]
  Sir, do you know how to go to Lujiazui?
- 师傅,请停在这里。[Shīfu, qǐng tíng zài zhèlǐ]
  Sir, please stop here.

Great, let's look at some examples to practice what we learned today.

- 请问，南京路怎么走？
  [Qǐng wèn, Nánjīng lù zěnme zǒu]
  Excuse me, how do you get to
  Nanjing Road?

- 对不起，我不认识路。
  [Duì bu qǐ, wǒ bú rènshí lù]
  Sorry, I don't know the road.

- 师傅，你知道怎么走吗？
  [Shīfu, nǐ zhīdào zěnme zǒu ma]
  Sir, do you know the way?

- 南京路在前边。
  [Nánjīng lù zài qiánbian]
  Nanjing Road is in the front.

- 请问，怎么买票？
  [Qǐng wèn, zěnme mǎi piào]
  Excuse me, how do you buy the ticket?

- 我坐 15 路车去上班。
  [Wǒ zuò 15 lù chē qù shàngbān]
  I will go to work by No.15 bus.

Great, so that wraps up today's lesson. Hope you have learned something. You can download our app to access all of our Chinese lessons. Learn Chinese anywhere, anytime with **ChineseAny**.

Word List

Main Vocabulary		
怎么[zěnme] how to	路[lù] road/bus number	师傅[shīfu] Sir(driver)

Notes

① 怎么 [zěnme] + **verb**：**how to**

　e.g. ● 你知道这个怎么做吗？［Nǐ zhīdào zhè ge zěnme zuò ma］

　　　　Do you know how to do this?

　　　● 中国饭怎么做？［Zhōngguó fàn zěnme zuò］

　　　　How to do Chinese food?

　　　● 请问,这里怎么走？［Qǐng wèn Zhèlǐ zěnme zǒu］

　　　　Excuse me, how do I get here?

　　　● 你们怎么回美国？［Nǐmen zěnme huí Měiguó］

　　　　How do you go back to America?

Quiz

I. Pronunciation.

　1. Please choose the initials or finals you heard.

　　1) A. lún　　　　　　　　　B. yún

　　2) A. bù　　　　　　　　　B. pù

　　3) A. é　　　　　　　　　　B. è

　　4) A. huài　　　　　　　　　B. guài

　2. Please choose the Pinyin you heard.

　　1) A. zěnme　　　　　　　　B. zhème

　　2) A. shàngcè　　　　　　　B. shàng chē

　　3) A. shīfu　　　　　　　　B. shūfu

　　4) A. xìqǔ　　　　　　　　　B. xīqǔ

II. Form sentences.

1. <u>qǐng</u> <u>shīfu</u> <u>zhège</u> <u>wèn</u> <u>lù</u> <u>zǒu</u> <u>zěnme</u>
    1   2   3   4   5   6   7

_____

2. <u>zěnme</u> <u>zhège</u> <u>Hànzì</u> <u>shuō</u>
    1   2   3   4

_____

3. <u>mǎi</u> <u>diànyǐng</u> <u>zěnme</u> <u>piào</u>
    1   2   3   4

_____

4. <u>Zhōngguó</u> <u>zhège</u> <u>cài</u> <u>zuò</u> <u>zěnme</u>
    1   2   3   4   5

_____

III. Please translate the following sentences into Chinese.

1. How do you know her phone number?

_____

2. I am on the way to work.

_____

3. I like to go to work on foot.

_____

4. How do you study Chinese?

_____

Go Straight, Please

Welcome to Level Three, Lesson Eighteen of our **ChineseAny** podcast series teaching Mandarin Chinese. Today we will learn three words: one adverb and two verbs. Let's look at them now.

The 1st character is adverb "*yìzhí* 一直", It has two meanings

➤ The 1st meaning is "straight".

Usually we use it before the VERB to express "go straight or directly".

一直
[yìzhí]
all the time   adjective

For example,

● 请一直走! [Qǐng yìzhí zǒu]
  Please go straight!

● 请一直上楼。[Qǐng yìzhí shànglóu]
  Please go upstairs straight.

➤ The 2nd meaning is "constantly/non-stop, all the time".

● 他一直说对不起。[Tā yìzhí shuō Duì bu qǐ]
  He constantly said sorry.

● 他一直在房间打电话。[Tā yìzhí zài fángjiān dǎ diànhuà]
  He kept making phone calls in the room.

● 我的车一直停在这儿。[Wǒ de chē yìzhí tíng zài zhèr]
  My car keeps parking here.

● 他今天早上一直喝咖啡。[Tā jīntiān zǎoshang yìzhí hē kāfēi]
  He had coffee all the time this morning.

The 2nd vocabulary is "*guǎi* 拐", Which means "to turn".

拐[guǎi]
to turn   verb

Previously we learned "*zuǒ* 左", left and "*yòu* 右", which means "right". So "*zuǒguǎi* 左拐", means "turn left" and "*yòuguǎi* 右拐", means "turn right".

When you take a taxi, you may often say the followings to the driver,

- 师傅，请左拐。[Shīfu, qǐng zuǒ guǎi]
  Sir, please turn left.

- 师傅，请右拐。[Shīfu, qǐng yòu guǎi]
  Sir, please turn right.

- 请不要在这儿拐。[Qǐng bú yào zài zhèr guǎi]
  Please don't turn here.

- 你怎么不拐？[Nǐ zěnme bù guǎi]
  Why didn't you turn?

OK, the 3rd vocabulary is "*diào tóu* 调头", "*diào tóu* 调头" is a verb, which means to do U-turn.

调头[diào tóu]
to U-turn   verb

For example：

- 请在前边调头。[Qǐng zài qiánbian diàotóu]
  Please do a U-turn in the front.

- 这儿不可以调头。[Zhèr bù kěyǐ diàotóu]
  You cannot do a U-turn here.

- 我们在哪儿调头？[Wǒmen zài nǎr diàotóu]
  Where shall we do a U-turn?

- 我们调头还是一直走？[Wǒmen diàotóu háishi yìzhí zǒu]
  Should we do a U-turn or go straight?

Great, let's look at some examples to practice what we have learned today.

- 我想一直在中国学习汉语。
  [Wǒ xiǎng yìzhí zài Zhōngguó xuéxí hànyǔ]
  I want to keep learning Chinese in China.

- 我们前边左拐。
  [Wǒmen qiánbian zuǒ guǎi]
  Let's turn left in the front.

- 我不知道左拐还是右拐。
  [Wǒ bù zhīdào zuǒ guǎi háishì yòu guǎi]
  I don't know whether to turn left or right.

- 我这个星期一直工作。
  [Wǒ zhège xīngqī yìzhí gōngzuò]
  I kept working this entire week.

- 他一直不在家。
  [Tā yìzhí bú zài jiā]
  He is out of home all the time.

- 我们可以调头吗？
  [Wǒmen kěyǐ diàotóu ma]
  Can we do a U-turn?

Great, so that wraps up today's lesson. Congratulations! You have made it to the last lesson of this level. You're making great progress and hope you have learnt something useful. Now that you have completed this level, please be sure to check out our practice library to test your comprehension this level. Download our app to access our Chinese lessons. As always, you can learn Chinese anywhere, anytime with **ChineseAny**.

Word List

Main Vocabulary		
一直[yìzhí] straight/continuously	拐[guǎi] turn	调头[diàotóu] do U-turn

Notes

① 一直[yìzhí]：straight；constantly/non-stop.

一直[yìzhí] **+ verb**

e.g. ● 师傅，我们一直走。[Shīfu, wǒmen yìzhí zǒu]

Sir, we go straight.

● 他一直不喜欢喝咖啡。[Tā yìzhí bù xǐhuan hē kāfēi]

He constantly does not like to drink coffee.

● 我们一直住在这里。[Wǒmen yìzhí zhù zài zhèlǐ]

We have constantly lived here.

Quiz

I. Pronunciation.

  1. Please choose the initials or finals you heard.

    1) A. zhào   B. jiào

    2) A. miǎo   B. niǎo

3) A. jì   B. qì

4) A. xiǎo   B. shǎo

2. Please choose the Pinyin you heard.

1) A. yìzhí   B. yízhì

2) A. zuǒ guǎi   B. zuòguài

3) A. yāoguài   B. yòu guǎi

4) A. zuǒyòu   B. zuòjiù

II. Form sentences.

1. nǐ   zhù   yìzhí   zài   ma   zhèlǐ
   1   2   3   4   5   6

_____

2. qiánbian   shīfu   qǐng   zuǒ   zài   guǎi
    1   2   3   4   5   6

_____

3. tā   shuō   yìzhí   duìbuqǐ
   1   2   3   4

_____

4. wǒ   máng   yìzhí   xīngqīliù   hěn
   1   2   3   4   5

_____

III. Please translate the following sentences into Chinese.

1. How did you know we turned left?

_____

2. Sir, we go straight.

_____

3. I constantly want to live in China.

_____

4. We turn right here.

_____